GOING BEYOND THE PIE GRAPH

TRUE DIVERSITY

Jesús Leal

with Nathan Hale Williams

ISBN: 978-1-09836-038-2 Print

ISBN: 978-1-09836-039-9 eBook

CONTENTS

Foreword

By Sherice Torres

Vice President of Marketing for F2 (Facebook Financial)

The year was 2004, and I was in the early years of my tenure as an executive at Nickelodeon. We were discussing the licensing potential for a new preschool show called The Backyardigans. Created by Janice Burgess, each episode highlighted the fantastical, imaginative backyard adventures of friends Austin (a kangaroo), Tasha (a hippo), Tyrone (a moose), and Uniqua (a one-of-a-kind character with an adventurous nature[1]). The conversation drifted towards character names, specifically Tyrone. Someone asked if the name was relatable enough to appeal to a broad audience. I must have made a face because my manager and long-time mentor, Leigh Anne Brodsky (then President of Nickelodeon Consumer Products), noticed my unease and questioned me about it.

"Sherice - you seem to have something on your mind. What do you think?"

I paused for a moment, then answered from the heart. "When I hear the name 'Tyrone', it reminds me of my Dad or my brother. The name feels like home."

With that one question, the course of the conversation changed. The Backyardigans went on to have a nearly decade-long run on Nick

Jr., with a successful line of preschool products sold around the globe. And while the success of the series (or related consumer products line) cannot be boiled down to one meeting, the conversation is a prime example of the power of TRUE DIVERSITY. Leigh Anne knew me well enough as a leader to catch even the most subtle cues. She recognized that I had a potentially dissenting and unspoken viewpoint to express in a critical business discussion. I was able to bring my unique perspective and Cultural Intelligence (or CQ) to the conversation, based upon my experience as a Black woman (not to mention the fact that the show's creator was also a Black woman). Finally, Leigh Anne created a culture of belonging where members of her team - from the most seasoned executives to those just starting out in their careers - felt comfortable sharing their perspectives and ideas, even if they varied from those of the larger group.

TRUE DIVERSITY goes beyond the pie chart metrics of racial and gender demographics to create a more holistic picture of the composition and culture of a company. In this timely and important book, Jesus Leal and Nathan Hale Williams break down each element of TRUE DIVERSITY - from hiring and retention to building Cultural Intelligence; identifying and combating bias, to avoiding and navigating diversity fatigue. Based upon the concept of DQ or the Diversity Quotient, TRUE DIVERSITY highlights the power of driving impact by focusing diversity & inclusion efforts on the totality of a person's experience - defined by who they really are beyond race and gender.

While not directly referenced in this work, TRUE DIVERSITY also addresses the critical concept of belonging. According to nonprofit think tank Coqual, "The concept of **belonging** is increasingly used in diversity and inclusion (D&I) work but hasn't been well-defined. ... **Belonging** at work means you feel seen for your unique contributions, connected to your coworkers, supported in your daily work and career development, and proud of your organization's values and purpose.[2]"

Leal and Williams drive home the point that a diverse workforce is only one part of the equation. Organizations must create an environment in which employees at all levels feel empowered and inspired to apply their unique perspectives and talents to address critical business challenges. Leaders must set the tone from the top that diversity and inclusion are business imperatives. Not nice-to-haves, but must-haves. Initiatives led exclusively by the HR team or Chief Diversity Officer are universally destined for failure. To achieve TRUE DIVERSITY, culture must be driven from the top, with a shared responsibility to foster a culture of belonging across all levels of the organization.

As a marketer by training, I operate with a near-obsessive focus on the customer. Success comes from centering on their needs, wants, and desires above all. No one cares about how cool your product or technology is - what really matters is, "What's in it for me?" How will this product make my life easier/help me achieve my goals/bring me closer to the things that I want/need/desire? Regardless of your industry, a business strategy that is not intensely focused on the needs and wants of your customer is a losing game. Likewise, TRUE DIVERSITY flips the perspective of an organization's D&I efforts from an internal to an external point of view. According to Leal and Williams:

"If you're looking to your customers as your guide in hiring, invariably you will create a diverse workforce. Very few businesses these days have a monolithic customer base. No consumer base is all white and all male. Therefore, instead of looking to hire X number of women or minorities, you should be looking to hire a workforce that reflects the needs and identity of your customer. Trust me, it will yield results that outpace any quota system or target numbers."

TRUE DIVERSITY is a must-read for leaders looking to create a competitive advantage, drive business results, and shift the culture of their organization as a whole. Leal and Williams bring the concept of TRUE DIVERSITY to life with a unique combination of independent research, case studies, and personal anecdotes from Leal's early life in Memorial Park, NJ, and decades-long career in the pharmaceutical industry.

Sherice Torres *is an inspirational leader with over 25 years of experience in marketing, brand management, strategic planning, and change management.*

Sherice Torres currently serves as the Vice President of Marketing for F2 (Facebook Financial), where she is responsible for all aspects of global marketing across Facebook's payments products including Facebook Pay and Novi. Previously, Sherice served in a variety of brand and product marketing roles at Google and Nickelodeon, including social responsibility, kids and family products, and inclusion. Sherice graduated magna cum laude from Harvard and earned her MBA at Stanford.

The Diversity of My Background

"Whether you know it or not, your desire to write comes from the urge to not just be creative, it's a need (one every human being on earth has) to help others." —Shawn Coyne

I was ready for the world, so I arrived early. I have been a fighter since day one, when I was born as a "preemie" in 1961 in communist Cuba—and I am still here to tell the story. My family name, Leal (which means "loyal"), is derived from a royal family of Seville, Spain. My family arrived in Cuba in a roundabout way, starting in Spain then emigrating to the Canary Islands and then to Cuba. Our journey didn't stop there—shortly after the revolution, my dad, Nilo, my mother, Rosa, my older brother, Luis, and I left everything behind in Cuba to seek asylum back in Spain. We landed in Spain literally with nothing—no clothes, no money. Nothing. The only thing my mother smuggled out of Cuba was a little gold icon of Jesus, which I still wear around my neck.

I was barely four pounds when I was born, and no one thought I was going to make it. We were in communist Cuba and there was no access to medicine, little access to infant formula, and not much food in general. The odds of my survival were very poor, and so they called me "Jesus Leal" ("Loyal to Jesus") and baptized me immediately because they believed my life could be short. "Thanks for the vote of confidence, mom and dad," I would often joke. But almost six decades later, here I am, doing quite well. Along the way, I have learned a lot about this world. From my birth until now, I can look back and see how every moment along my journey has shaped both my worldview and who I am today. My never-give-up spirit started on day one, and my understanding of how to interact with people from a wide range of backgrounds is derived directly from the experiences I have had, starting all the way back in childhood.

As I said, when my family fled Cuba, we arrived in Spain in the middle of the summer. My dad wanted to memorialize our freedom, so he paid a photographer to take the picture below. Please note the oversized and extremely heavy coats that we'd been given by the church's clothing donation to wear in August 1965.

(Image 1)

We had to wait in Spain for four months while the United States government vetted my parents' eligibility for asylum. During those times, there was a heightened concern that Cubans were trying to infiltrate the US with communist ideas or, worse yet, act as spies for the communist government.

We struggled in Spain for four months. We left Cuba with only three pieces of clothing each and no money. Spaniards would not hire Cubans because they knew that we would pick up and leave the jobs as soon as we would get approved to come to America. Having no money, our only source of food was a homeless shelter but we were only allowed to eat after the homeless Spaniards were fed. Some days there was no food left after the homeless were fed so we would go hungry on those days. My father's brother, Rodolfo Leal who fled Cuba to the US just two years earlier, was able to wire just enough money to pay for one bedroom in a Madrid hostel.

In order to start the process of immigrating legally to the US, my uncle was required to submit a sworn affidavit attesting to the fact that he had paid for an apartment in the US and could provide work for both of my parents. After the sworn affidavit (attesting to the fact that there were jobs at embroidery factories for both of my parents) was received by the US Embassy in Spain, the vetting/background check was allowed to move towards completion and the process of coming to America began to materialize.

NEW JERSEY, USA & MEMORIAL PARK

Back in Cuba, my parents were professional educators, teaching at the equivalent level of high school AP classes and early college curricula. When we arrived in America, however, both of my parents had to get jobs as factory workers because they didn't know the language. We settled in a town called West New York, New Jersey. It was 1965, and West New York had been predominantly settled by Italian,

Polish, and Irish immigrants. There were very few African-Americans or Hispanics when we landed in the Hudson County area of New Jersey, but the numbers of Hispanics were growing rapidly. The area consisted of West New York, North Bergen, Guttenburg, Weehawken, and Union City. Union City was the textile capital of the US so there was plenty of unskilled labor work, and my parents both found jobs in the embroidery business.

My parents spent the majority of their time working, so my Dad tried to find ways to ensure we didn't get into any trouble. His thought was that if he kept our minds busy, we would not have any time to get into trouble. My adoptive parent became a place called Memorial Park. I talk a lot about Memorial Park because it is there that I learned many of the fundamental life lessons that have guided me in life—it was also the birthplace of many of the theories that I have developed and which form the basis for this book.

West New York was an interesting town to grow up in for a young boy from Cuba. You walked everywhere. You walked to school. You walked to the grocery store. You walked to church. And you walked to the park. Walking everywhere was so common that my mother never learned how to drive. That was a uniqueness of the town and the community that is almost impossible to find elsewhere. My brother and I got involved in everything from ice skating, basketball, football, marbles, you name it; all at Memorial Park. For me, I played everything except baseball. I think I am the only Cuban who doesn't like baseball. But there's a reason.

My older brother, Luis, was one of those kids who started shaving in the third grade. He was always big for his age, refused to wear his glasses, and always seemed older than he was. He loved to drag me along with him to play stickball, and being the younger brother, I didn't have a choice. He also loved to pitch inside the batter's box and would often hit me with the ball, which I did not love. He hit me so many times, in fact, that I knew I had to choose a different sport. That's when I decided to play football. Why? So, I could actually hit back. One of those invaluable life lessons learned in Memorial Park: play the game that does not make you a victim and gives you the opportunity to win.

Another life lesson that I carry through my professional life—and one of the reasons I am writing this book—is this: tell your own story, or someone else will tell it for you.

We met a bunch of kids, ages seven through nine, when we first started going to Memorial Park. As part of the initiation ritual, the older kids would pick out a nickname for you, and that would be your nickname for all time, like it or not. It wasn't just childhood hazing, though; there was some practicality to it. There were about twenty Jose's in that park, so you needed a way to figure out about which Jose you were talking.

My friend Manny was given the nickname Culo de Vaca, which translates to a "cow's ass"—presumably because he had a big rear end for a small kid. My friend Jorge was given the nickname Cara de Jeva, which means "chick's face." I saw how this was going, so when they got to me and asked me what my nickname was, I replied, "Chuwy." And they stopped, looked at me, and said, "Okay, that's cool." Chuwy became my nickname, and I wasn't embarrassed to carry it through my life because I had picked it myself. Know who you are and tell your own story.

LEARNING DIVERSITY LESSONS IN SCHOOL

In contrast to the jocular environment of Memorial Park, my parents enrolled my brother and me in Catholic school, which was remarkable because they barely had enough money to pay the rent. Notwithstanding their limited resources, they put us in Catholic school because in 1965 there was an influx of refugees into West New York, so the public-school system became really crowded. In order to deal with the overcrowding, the school system began what was known as split school days. Half of the

9

students went to school in the morning, and the other half went to school in the afternoon. As you can imagine, my dad did not like that idea—too much free time. To him, a half-day to ourselves meant more opportunities for trouble, so my parents sacrificed and worked even harder for our education. And to keep us out of trouble.

The Catholic school was tiny. It had only one classroom per grade level (in contrast to the public school, which had multiple classrooms per grade). Out of the twenty or so kids in my class, I was one of three boys who were minorities. There were a few more minority girls in my class than males, but the white students were the clear majority. I remember there was only one black female student; she was also of Cuban descent. Even though the demographics of my grammar school were different than those of Memorial Park, the minorities all stuck together by the nature of the size of the school. We still even meet for reunions forty-plus years later.

I had to develop an ability to get along with my friends at school as well as my friends at Memorial Park, most of whom attended the crowded public schools. For many minorities, it is a skill that has to be learned at a very early age: the ability to survive in a broad range of environments and situations.

It was a skill set that I further cultivated in high school. I went to Catholic school until the eighth grade, at which point I basically said to my parents, "Save your money, Memorial High School is massive but not overcrowded." My graduating class was well over nine hundred students, and I had the fortunate opportunity to interact with a truly diverse set of students. I was an honors student and socialized with the "smart kids" in my classes. Since I loved sports, I also hung out with the jocks and athletes. My experiences in Memorial Park even allowed me to relate to and befriend the kids that often got in trouble. It was truly "inclusive" before anyone was using the term.

By the time I entered my last year of high school, I was elected the student body president because I had developed the ability to reach across a broad range of social groups, so much so that I won the election in a landslide. I received votes from the smart kids in my classes, the kids that I had tutored and helped with their studies, the athletes who I played ball with, and the kids who I drank $2 wine with in the park. (And this was not Two Buck Chuck quality, either). I had an expansive perspective that covered the entire student body, and this afforded me the ability to relate to the most diverse cross-section. I was able to get along with everybody and anybody because I understood and respected their point of view.

In West New York, you really didn't have much of a choice except to interact with everyone—no matter their race, background, skill level, or economic status. The entire town was one square mile, so you were geographically forced to engage. At that time, I believe it was one of the most heavily populated square miles in the United States, based on the census. You certainly didn't have the option to isolate yourself based on perceived differences. In fact, our differences were the bedrock of the community and what made it such a rich environment in which to mature.

I also learned during that time the distinct difference between the pressures put on men and women in the workforce. My mother tells the story about how she cried for a week when she found out she was pregnant with my younger sister, Lourdes. She was upset that she would lose her job. (At that time, it was not an uncommon practice for an employer to fire a laborer because of a leave of absence, such as a pregnancy. Thank God for new laws such as Family Leave Laws!) Our family depended on both incomes from my father and my mother, and she knew we could not afford for her to lose her job. I didn't learn of this story until I was a young adult, and imagining the conflict that it put her under still has an effect on me. She was excited to have another child, yet she was deeply anxious about her ability to continue to help my father provide for our family. Although the laws have changed, this remains a common dilemma for working mothers, which I have often taken into consideration in the workforce.

Beyond the great lessons about inclusivity that high school taught me, my time there also impacted me in other important ways. One life-changing event that impacted me in high school years was my science teacher, Mr. Louis Marchesani. Mr. Marchesani wore many hats, one of which was being the faculty adviser to the officers of the student body. Another hat that Mr. Marchesani wore was as a local pharmacist. He taught at the high school during the school year, and while on summer break, he would work as a pharmacist down on the Jersey Shore.

Mr. Marchesani and I had developed a mentor relationship as a result of his advisory role to the student body officers. During my junior year, the economy experienced a downturn, which prompted him to tell me, "With gas prices, unemployment, and interest rates rising, you need an education and a job that requires a license, like a pharmacist." His rationale was that "if the economy gets better, there will be a lot of competition for jobs. You need a career that requires a license so that it limits the pool of potential applicants. No one can do the job of a pharmacist without a pharmacist license." Unbeknownst to him, I had a strong interest in medicine, but I did not want to practice medicine. I had been a great student up until then, but it was the discovery of pharmacy that got me more excited about school. My new goal was to go to pharmacy school for college.

My dad made the choice of going to college pretty simple. He was a direct and straightforward man with three basic rules.

One: you decide to do something that got you
in trouble with the law—out of my house

Two: you decide to mess up with your grades
and leave school—out of my house

Three: you get a girl pregnant—out of my house

I appreciated his simplicity because there was no room for misunderstanding. I was going to college, not getting in trouble, and definitely not getting a girl pregnant.

Remember, my parents were both educators in Cuba. It was a given that not only was I going to college, I was going to graduate from college. I made the decision to go to Rutgers University primarily for financial reasons. It was the state university, and they had a great pharmacy school. Because I'd done well in high school, I was able to secure enough scholarship money and financial aid that paid for the entire five years. It was important to me that I wasn't a burden to my parents financially. I ended up living at home for most of the five years until I graduated.

KEY LIFE LESSONS AT RUTGERS' PHARMACY SCHOOL

Naturally, I learned a lot about being a pharmacist in school, however, college was about more than just the classroom. At our twenty-fifth reunion of Pharmacy School, I walked up to one of my professors and said to his wife, "You know, your husband didn't teach me a lot about science." The whole table went quiet. Mind you, I was speaking to one of the most esteemed professors from Rutgers' Pharmacy School. They had to be thinking, what nerve this young man has to have to insult this incredible professor! Then I said, "Don't get me wrong. Dr. Medwick did teach me a lot about science. The reason why I say that he did not teach me much about science is because he taught me a lot more about life, and that dwarfed what he taught me in science." Not only did I ease the tension at the table, Dr. Medwick gave me a big hug and said, "Thank you, not many students get that."

Dr. Medwick was notoriously the hardest professor in the Pharmacy School, with the two most dreaded classes: Analytical Chemistry I ("AC1") and Analytical Chemistry II ("AC2"). These two classes were what we called the "weed-out classes." After one or both of these classes, many young pharmacy students would leave the school with their tail between their legs, looking for another major. Either you made it through these classes, or you didn't make it through pharmacy school. Not only did I make it through both semesters, Dr. Medwick came to me at the end of Analytical Chemistry II to tell me, "You are in a select group of people who have aced both of the semesters."

Later, Dr. Medwick approached me again to inquire about my summer plans. "Dr. Medwick," I explained, "I'm not like the rest of the kids in pharmacy school. I can't intern at a pharmacy. I need to make a lot of money in the summer to pay for the next year. The only way I can earn that amount of money is working two jobs, loading trucks and being a short-order cook."

Dr. Medwick looked at me and laughed. "I want you to consider working at Hoffman-La Roche for the summer in the analytical chemistry department," he said matter-of-factly.

"With all due respect Dr. Medwick, how much does it pay?" I asked.

He laughed again—even harder. I don't recall the exact amount of money, but it was at least two or three times what I would make loading trucks and having a second job as a short-order cook. It was also in my field of study and would intellectually challenge me. I'm certainly glad Dr. Medwick persisted because I would have missed another life-changing opportunity.

These stories demonstrate how Dr. Medwick was a real mentor to me. He saw my potential and ability, which made him want to take me under his wing. There's a saying I love that he embodied: most human beings don't fail because they set the bar too high and miss hitting the high bar, they fail because they set the bar too low and hit it. Dr. Medwick set the bar extremely high to see if we could hit the top. That summer job was what led me into the pharmaceutical industry, and it would forever change my career path.

So, in the summer of 1983, I took the summer job at Hoffman-LaRoche. I was assigned two projects that were supposed to last the entire summer. The FDA ordered the first, and the most important, project. The goal was to develop assays to carefully quantify the amount of inactive ingredients in different formulations. The first formulation that I worked on was for an antibiotic suspension using a method called the High-Performance Liquid Chromatography ("HPLC"). The funny thing is that as complicated as that sounds, I solved the issue while drinking a Diet Coke.

I had a list of the ingredients that I needed to quantify from the antibiotic suspension. While drinking a Diet Coke, I noticed that some of the inactive ingredients in my suspension were also listed as ingredients in Diet Coke. Remember, 1983 was pre-internet, so you had one of two choices: 1) go to the library or 2) ask someone. I picked up the phone, called Coca Cola, and asked to speak to someone from quality control. How did I get through to them? Because I was working in the quality control department of a big pharma company. I guess the internal sirens went off because the request to speak to quality control led to a very long hold times with multiple people until a senior QC person returned to the call.

The Head of Quality Control was the fifth or sixth person I had spoken to by then. "Is there a problem?" he asked.

"No, there's no problem. I never said there was a problem. I am a pharmacy student looking to speak to someone about quality control," I corrected him.

Relieved, he replied, "By the time the message got to me, it sounded like there was a major problem. How can I help you?"

"I'm supposed to separate these ingredients and I need to know if there's any published literature that I can use to help me with my project."

Within a few minutes, he provided me with public references of studies that may help me separate the ingredients that I had to work with, such as solubility, pH, column types, column lengths, and so on. The information I received from Coca-Cola helped me finish the project within a week of starting the internship.

The second project took about a week-and-a-half for me to finish, but I still had the entire summer to finish out my internship. I was paid a lump-sum stipend, so they had to find something for me to do for the remainder of the summer. As a result, I was allowed to rotate between many departments: toxicology, crystallography, animal health. Finally, I landed in the sales department after seemingly exhausting all chemistry-related ones.

I found it interesting to see what they were doing in the sales training, so I asked to do a ride-a-long with one of the field sales representatives. I was so poor that I had to borrow a suit so I could join him in the field. The rotation in sales excited me about the business side of pharmaceuticals. Dr. Medwick had sent me to Hoffmann-LaRoche to get interested in a PhD in Analytical Chemistry, and here I was, about to tell him that I wanted an MBA instead. For a poor kid from Cuba, the business side of Pharma caught my attention as much as the chemistry side.

DISCOVERING DIVERSITY ISSUES IN PHARMA

After pharmacy school, I got my first job in pharmaceutical sales in Newark. I know that one of the reasons I was hired was because in my cover letter to the manager, Sue Talley (who was the first female manager in the company's history), I wrote the following: "To work in Newark, not only do you need to understand the science like all of the representatives, you need to understand the streets." Back then, I don't think I fully understood the wisdom of that simple statement. I was just posturing to get the job, which I did.

At Schering-Plough, I excelled in sales. I was the top sales representative during the launch of a new product, Normodyne. I was also the top salesman for all products combined. I became one of the very first regional field trainers. After two years, I became the youngest District Sales Manager in Schering-Plough history. Over the next four years, I turned two districts around from "bottom of the barrel to cream of the crop."

I completed my graduate studies and earned a Masters in Business Administration from Nova University in Fort Lauderdale, Florida. Once I finished the MBA, I thought I would be a shoo-in for promotions to the main headquarters and various management roles. Wow, was I mistaken. Up to that point, I had not felt any kind of discrimination. Was it because the level that I was at was an "appropriate/acceptable level" for a minority or maybe I was just too young or naïve to fully understand what was happening? Time and time again, I was passed up for jobs in favor of less-qualified and less-successful colleagues. I was a better sales person, a better trainer, a Registered Pharmacist in two states and an MBA. Even with all of my qualifications, I would not even get an interview for a job in the home office. After one such instance, another co-worker said to me, "Jesús, they're afraid of you in HQ." Afraid of me? Why? I didn't understand it. It would take years for me to understand that I was experiencing the same thing as a wise, successful Cuban entrepreneur I once knew, who told me:

"A nosotros nos mastican pero no nos tragan."
The literal translation: "They will chew on us but not swallow."

After being passed for multiple opportunities, I was recruited by a minority recruiter, Levi Jordan, for a startup company, Boehringer Mannheim Pharmaceuticals Corporation (BMPC). I immediately hit it off when my soon-to-be boss, Larry Summerville, an extremely intelligent African-American gentleman who was also an incredible guy.

Many people questioned my decision to leave Schering-Plough (where I had eight years of success) to move to a startup that had no guarantees. A quote from James Conant kept going through my head when I was contemplating the decision: "Behold the turtle. He makes great strides when he sticks his neck out." I stuck my neck out and took the chance.

A year later, Larry said to me, "One day, you'll probably be my boss. That's why I know I made a great decision in hiring you." I told him to stop trying to make me feel good with the psychological motivation, to which he replied, "No, I'm being serious. Unlike the bosses of the past, I'm not afraid of you. I like when you challenge me. I like when you come up with different ideas. That is why we need diversity."

Larry's statement about not being afraid of me immediately connected to my experience at the previous company. My previous employers were afraid of me because I represented high competency wrapped in a minority package. It was the first time in my career that I realized that I might have to change my approach solely because I come from a racial minority background. I didn't like the idea, but I knew it was something I had to consider if I was going to continue to succeed in a corporate environment.

As Larry predicted, the startup grew, and although I did not become his boss, I eventually had more responsibilities than he did. We moved into different areas of the business, and to Larry's credit, there was never any animosity or hard feelings toward my rise in the company. He truly was one of the greatest leaders I have ever worked with, and he was an amazing identifier of talent—after all, he had predicted my success years in advance.

Larry was more experienced and wiser than me. What he could not have predicted (and maybe more important, communicated with me in a meaningful way) were the challenges that I would face as I continued to climb the corporate ladder. Boehringer Mannheim Pharmaceuticals Corporation was purchased by Hoffman-LaRoche (HLR) and I joined

HLR. I was hoping for a similar role to the one I had but no chance! I took a role about 3 levels lower than what I had at BMPC, I became the Head of Sales for Oncology and Dermatology. Although it was a much lower-level position than I had previously held-it turned out to be one of the most rewarding decisions that I have ever made. I was working for a great company and was given great opportunities to prove myself on much bigger jobs. It also taught me the necessity of understanding your customer base and the importance of having diverse perspectives on your team for ideation and innovation.

Frank Condella, one of the most intelligent and amazing executives in the pharmaceutical industry, hired me to work for Roche to run the oncology and dermatology sales groups. Frank was also a pharmacist with an MBA, so I believe that he took a liking to the fact that we followed similar paths. He and his family are also very religious and perhaps my name endeared him – just kidding. Bottom line, a true gentleman of the highest ethical character. I enjoyed great success launching Xeloda for breast cancer and leading the sales efforts for Accutane in severe acne. A year after I started, Frank surprised me by asking me to take over the entire hepatitis franchise of the company. This opportunity included direct reports in Sales, Marketing, PR, and Medical. I was also managing a matrixed organization that included Market Research, Market Access, Philanthropy, Legal, HR, and others. Oddly enough, I replaced an individual to whom I had reported at Schering-Plough, and to whom I had handed my resignation letter when I left that company. I take no pride in this; I just want to highlight how important it is to understand how small this world really is.

I was enjoying early success at Roche, and at the six-month mark, Frank left the company to take on a CEO role at another Pharma company. Who can blame him? Frank's replacement was Georges Gemayel. Georges is a Christian Lebanese PhD and an extremely smart guy. In addition to being smart, Georges was charismatic and opinionated. Georges and I clashed like titans when we first met. It was through these clashes that he and I developed our mutual respect. Today, if Georges ever called me for a role, I would drop everything and join him.

On Georges's first night in the United States, he kept our entire team until 11 p.m. This was challenging, as I am not a night person. Typically, I get into the office early, and that day I'd arrived at 5:45 a.m., which made it a 17-hour day. Needless to say, I didn't hide my feelings well, as I have never been known to have a good poker face. I told you that Georges was a very smart guy, so there was no doubt in my mind that he knew that I was upset.

The next morning, I arrived at my cubical at 6:45 a.m. (just in case it would be another long night) only to find Georges sitting on an upside-down trash can in front of my desk. I looked at him. He looked at me. I said, "What? You greet me this early and you don't bring coffee?" That was my way of breaking the ice and showing my respect that he had shown up early to speak with me. We've had an incredible relationship ever since.

Because Georges was Lebanese, he deeply understood the differences amongst minority communities, and this opened the door for what I really wanted to do with our product for Hepatitis C. We were entering a market that Schering-Plough had dominated for over fifteen years. Roche had tried previously to get a foot in the door of the Hepatitis C (HCV) market, and failed miserably with the launch of Roferon-A.

I knew that in order to penetrate the HCV market and gain market share, we could not execute a traditional launch. Hepatitis C is a discriminating disease. Socio-economic factors play a role in infection rates. Once infected, the time from diagnosis to treatment is longer for minorities. The longer a patient waits for treatment, the greater the progression of disease and the lower the response to treatment. In other words, minorities are not diagnosed as early as non-minorities, once diagnosed the time to start treatment is significantly longer for minorities so the status of the liver is worse and the outcomes suffer. Because HCV does not affect everyone the same way, we could not approach it the same way that we approached other drug launches. I looked at this as an opportunity, and I assembled the most diverse team of pharmaceutical professionals that have ever launched a major brand (non-scientific opinion). I did not want to hire resumes—in fact, most people on the team were NOT experienced in the critical roles that they were hired to fill. I wanted to hire people who really wanted to make a change in peoples' lives. In order to do so, we had to have a team full of the freshest ideas coming from truly diverse backgrounds.

WALKING THE WALK AND TALKING THE TALK – TRUE DIVERISTY

Nationality/Education Discipline	Yrs of Marketing Exp Prior to Joining the Pegasys Team	Industry Position Prior to Joining the Pegasys Team	Position on Pegasys Team
Turkish/Engineer	0	Market Analyst	Product Manager
Greek /Physician	0	Transplant Hepatologist	Medical Director
Armenian/Pharmacist	0	Clinical Pharmacist	Product Manager
American/Pharmacist	0	Clinical Pharmacist	Product Manager
Chinese/Business	0	Market Analyst	Product Director
American/Business	0	Supply Chain	Product Director
Lebanese/Physician	0	Physician Infectious Diseases	Medical Director
Lebanese PhD Pharmacy	10	Country Head	VP Specialty
Egyptian/Pharmacist	0	Pharmacy Intern	Clinical Specialist Manager
American/Engineer	0	Engineer	Product Manager

African American/Business	0	Operations	Multi-Cultural Marketing
Spaniard/Physician	0	Transplant Surgeon	Medical Director
Cuban/Pharmacist	0	Sales Director	VP Franchise
German/Business	0	Product Manager	Sales Director
American /Finance	10	Marketing Director	Marketing Director
Dominican/Business	5	Marketing Director	Marketing Director
African American/Business	0	Sales Director	Sales Director
African American/Business	0	Sales Director	Sales Director

(Table 1)

Our team also had to understand the characteristics, impediments to care and other factors of our target population in order to effectively launch the drug and reach patients that need it the most. We enlisted a community organizer and businesswoman, Joyce Rayzer, who was on the ground to partner with us in developing a program that was tailored specifically for the target population (minorities in either inner cities or extremely rural areas with little to no access to diagnostic and treatment options)

Today, Joyce continues to champion the causes of the minority populations as they relate to health, wealth disparities, and social determinants—all areas that brand teams still refuse to confront in their business plans! Some of the limitations of the target population were the lack of early detection and access to treatment due to travel and geographic limitations.

Because we worked with a diverse team and tapped into the needs as well as the limits of the target population, we were able to ideate an innovative program called Hope-C that was independently run by The Morehouse School of Medicine and Howard University. The purpose of the program was to educate nurses to identify HCV earlier and bring treatment options to patients where there were no HCV treaters. It was one of the most successful launches in my career, and I largely credit our success to the diversity of my team.

DIVERSITY LESSONS I LEARNED BEING A "GIRL DAD"

Many of the lessons that have impacted my success came from outside of the office. I got married and started a family along the way. I was blessed to have three beautiful daughters who have taught me more about life than any job could. I joke that God didn't give me any boys because I'd be too hard on them, just like my parents were on my brother and me. Instead, having three girls forced me to sit back and try to understand women and girls. I started reading about girls and how to be better at raising them by understanding the differences in our communication styles. It was completely different than the way I was raised, and so it was a unique learning experience for me. I approached it as a chance for me to become a better person overall. It had the intended effect.

When my girls were really young, I decided to start coaching girls' basketball. I figured that I didn't know much about girls, but I knew a lot about basketball. I signed them up for every sport that I could think of, hoping it would help me connect with them further. I also wanted to keep them busy (like my dad), so my girls played basketball, tee-ball, and soccer. Then, sometime around the ages of 13, 12, and 10, all three of them got interested in competitive cheerleading. And so yes, I became a cheer dad. Talk about the unexpected.

Being a cheer dad taught me so much more than I would have imagined. My girls weren't your standard cheerleaders. They were competitive cheerleaders in a league of their own. They won the national championship in Myrtle Beach two years in a row. They missed a year, and then came back to win the next, with my oldest as one of their coaches. In the end, they were three-time national champion competitive cheerleaders. Needless to say, I was a very proud cheer dad.

My daughters' participation in competitive cheer completely changed my viewpoint about girls and women, particularly when it comes to competition. I learned that women and girls could be greater competitors than men and boys, and a hell of a lot tougher. There are far more injuries in competitive cheerleading than there are in baseball, basketball, and football combined. I also learned about the need to develop a "winning mindset" and what happens if you allow doubt to enter your thoughts. I learned this from the "pre-routine" chant they did whenever they took to the mat: "Star Athletics, back with a mission, we'll take the title and we don't need permission." Wow! You should have seen the look on the faces of the teams that were coming up next. It had not occurred to me at the time, but this team was a good example of diversity. You had White, Black, Hispanic, Asian, and so on. What united them all was their strong work ethic and their desire to win.

Over the years, from my experiences at Memorial Park to my various executive and management positions to the lessons I learned from my family, I have had a unique experience watching how diversity and gender, as well as other factors such as age and sexual orientation, have impacted the workplace. I will continue to share those experiences and anecdotes throughout this book to illustrate and underscore my points. We have all heard the pitch for diversity, and it is well-settled that a diverse workforce is directly related to a company's bottom line and overall success. Still, I believe that many companies and organizations miss the mark by basing their diversity and inclusion strategies solely on characteristics found on a pie graph. This simplistic, generalized view is perhaps the most insulting characterization of a diverse workforce.

A pie chart or graph is a type of graph that displays data in a circular form. It is intended to be used as a quick visual representation of variables and factors. A pie graph represents a part-to-whole relationship of data. It is one of the most widely used and misused types of data visualizations. Each segment of the graph represents one component and all slices added together equal the whole. Humans gravitate to circles as the universal symbol of unity, perfection, and infinity. Ideally, we prefer for things to be whole—and understand how the respective pieces relate to the whole. Therein lies the problem with using a pie graph when it comes to diversity. It only provides a part of the story.

One thing is clear from my life and career: you cannot get the totality of someone's background from their resume or the boxes they check on an application. I am more than Cuban. I am more than a kid from an industrial town in New Jersey. I am more than a chemist. I am more than an experienced salesman, manager, and executive. I am more than a proud husband and father. I am all of those things plus so much more. And to truly understand who I am and my potential value to a company, you must go beyond the pie graph. It is a two-dimensional tool that is intended to address a multi-dimensional issue. We are not an island of penguins, we are not all the same, so we should stop minimizing our differences by showing a pie graph to support the claim that an organization is diverse.

In this book, I make the case for the necessity and benefit of applying my principles and approach to finding a truly diverse workforce. I will echo many of the prevailing theories from the lens of my own understanding and experience. I will also put forth novel ideas around the theories of diversity and inclusion planning, hiring, and implementation. I rely on real-life scenarios as the basis for my theories that will indeed help you and your teams ideate, innovate, and outperform the marketplace using a diverse workforce as a cornerstone to your success.

CHAPTER 1:

True Diversity Defined

"Diversity: the art of thinking independently together."
—Malcolm Forbes

Diversity and its sister, inclusion, are two words that are heard over and over again in the corporate marketplace and throughout our daily conversations. Even Hollywood has taken up the Diversity & Inclusion ("D&I") gauntlet in its hiring practices and the decisions about which projects are produced. D&I is a burgeoning area for consultants, specialists, and in-house corporate teams. Even with all of the talk around these two very familiar words, if you ask two people what either means, you will likely get two very different answers. More importantly, if you ask ten people what a successful D&I program or plan looks like, you'll likely get twenty different answers, most of which will be centered around the two-dimensional statistics of race and gender.

My goal is not to confuse the matter any further. Instead, I want to add insight on what I have to come know is a successful diversity plan, one that represents TRUE DIVERSITY and a multi-dimensional approach to the issue. Let's first start with some definitions that are common in the D&I zeitgeist. Then, I'll provide my definition of TRUE DIVERSITY accompanied by some anecdotal and analytical support.

The chapter ends with my four takeaways that I want you to remember throughout reading this book.

Merriam Webster's Dictionary defines diversity as "the condition of having or being composed of differing elements, variety, especially: the inclusion of different types of people (such as people of different races or cultures) in a group or organization."[3] D&I consultants and experts, Mark Kaplan and Mason Donovan, define it as the following: "[Diversity] is the presence of difference. It can be measured, tracked, and recorded. There are self-identifying differences, which are more difficult to put into a spreadsheet…."[4] (The qualifier of this definition is the basis of my principles around TRUE DIVERSITY.)

The University of North Carolina at Chapel Hill posed this question, "How would you define diversity?" in an open-ended survey to their student body in April 2010. No two answers were the same. Here are some of the responses:

- A wide range of interests, backgrounds, experiences.

- Differences among groups of people and individuals based on ethnicity, race, socioeconomic status, gender, exceptionalities, language, religion, sexual orientation, and geographical areas.

- Diversity can be measured across many variables—age, race, sex, economics, geography, religion, philosophy, etc.

- Anything that sets one individual apart from another. However, often it is used to specifically reference gender, race, ethnicity, and more recently, sexual orientation differences.

- Diversity is the immersion and comprehensive integration of various cultures, experiences, and people.

- Oh, a hard questionnaire, is it?[5]

The last response is one of my favorites, not just for its humor but because it encapsulates the complexity of diversity and why it can be difficult for companies to develop and implement successful D&I programs.

David A. Livermore, PhD, is a noted social scientist, devoted to the topics of cultural intelligence (CQ) and global leadership. His definition of diversity is also informative to this discussion: Here is the definition submitted by one of the respondents:

> "Diversity is sometimes used to broadly include any kind of difference, such as differences in personality, skills, working styles, tenure and thinking. But if diversity includes everything, it ends up meaning nothing. On the other hand, diversity is more than just black versus white or German versus Chinese. Each of us is part of several different social groups, and there's incredible diversity within most countries."[6]

With all of the diversity amongst the definitions (see what I did there), one thing is common to them all. No definition presents it as two-dimensional, which is how I believe too many companies see diversity today. A two-dimensional look at diversity based solely on race and gender can easily be captured on a page or in a pie graph, and for that reason, it's easy. Easy, however, does not usually lend itself to great innovation or overall success.

True diversity, however, is multi-dimensional and cannot be simply captured on a page or in a pie graph. In addition to race and gender, looking at an organization through a truly diverse lens forces you to examine the dimensions of time (when someone was born), space (where someone was born), and something that I call the Diversity Quotient, or "DQ." A person's DQ captures the totality of their experiences that define who they really are beyond their race or gender.

DIVERSITY QUOTIENT (DQ)

A quotient is a mathematical statement or formula where you obtain a result by dividing one quantity by another.[7] In my DQ fraction, the denominator captures as many factors affecting who you are, such as time, geographical location of where you were born, where you have lived, where you currently live, your socio-economic status, politics and policies that affect your day-to-day life, and other environmental factors that impact your worldview aside from race and gender. In the numerator, you only include those factors where you experienced a direct interaction with and/or were significantly influenced by those factors. Put another way, did you effectively experience the factors in the denominator so that they had an impact on your worldview? If so, it goes into the numerator.

In mathematical terms, if you were to have experienced everything happening in the world, society, and your community or group, you would have a DQ quotient of 1. Then apply that number times 100 to result in a DQ score of up to 100. See Images 2.1 - 2.3.

$DQ_{(i)}$: Diversity Quotient (Individual)

$$DQ_{(i)} = PIPSE_{(t)}/APSE_{(t)} \times 100$$

Diversity Quotient = Personal Impacting Political, Social, Economic Events$_{(t)}$ / All Political, Social, Economic Events$_{(t)}$

(t) = bound by same time frame

Score can theoretically range from 0-100.

At zero, the individual would have to be totally insulated from everything around him/herself. At one hundred, the individual would have to be fully impacted by every single event that was occurring at that time, and place. Both extremes are basically impossible to achieve.

(Image 2.1)

DQ: Diversity Quotient Example

A personal example of how two Cubans living in the same time and place (1959 circa Cuba's Revolution), can have very different Diversity Quotients:

Cuban A:
- Joined the Fidelista Group, supported the revolution
- Previously owned no property, land or business
- Lived the next 50 years as a Communist supporter and lived somewhat similar to how he lived before the revolution

Cuban B:
- Did not support the revolution
- Owned a business – business is taken over by the government
- Owned land and a home that had been passed down over generations - the government destroys the title to his house, confiscates his bank accounts as all his property is seized by the state
- His family organizes a protest with other families - results in imprisonment as "enemies of the revolution"
- After 2 years of hard labor, he decides to leave everything behind and flee with his family to Spain for political asylum
- Eventually they make it to the US, no family here, do not speak the language, no money, no social programs for aid, no health insurance etc.

Therefore, Cuban A & B are surrounded by the same $APSE_{(t)}$. However, Cuban B's $PIPSE_{(t)}$, the number of personally impacting events are significantly higher Cuban A, resulting in a higher.

A standard, Diversity Pie Graph would credit 1 Hispanic for each Cuban A and Cuban B. However, a True Diversity accounting would see these two as two very different Cubans based on their experiences. Those experiences shape the way we interpret data, make decisions etc.

(Image 2.2)

$DQ_{(g)}$: Diversity Quotient (group)

$DQ_{(g)}$ = Summation of all the individual $DQ_{(i)}$ w/in a group

$$DQ_{(g)} = \sum_{(t)}^{n} (DQ_{(i)1} + DQ_{(i)2} + DQ_{(i)3} \cdots\cdots DQ_{(i)n})$$

Where = $DQ_{(i)}$ = $PIPSE_{(t)}$/$APSE_{(t)}$ x 100 for each member of group

Σ: summation of all individual $DQ_{(t)}$ w/in a group

(Image 2.3)

Clearly, no one experiences one hundred percent of these many social, cultural, and economic factors, so all of us fall somewhere on this DQ spectrum. Important to note that this formula can demonstrate how a non-minority (based simply on race) can be more diverse than someone from a so-called racial minority. On the other side, if you are someone living in a bubble, then your score will be closer to zero.

The DQ concept is best illustrated in examples. Take someone born in Cuba in the 1950s through the early 1960s. During that time, Cuba was transitioning from one of the wealthiest nations in the Caribbean to what would ultimately become a communist government when Castro rose to power in 1959. Castro did not announce himself as a communist when he was enrolling people to fight Batista, so people trusted him. It was only after he took control of the government a couple of years later that he announced his communist intentions, and then began to take away land and businesses. In this example, if you were born just twenty years later, you only know communist Cuba and not the Cuba before Castro. A Cuban born in 1981 has a distinctly different DQ regarding Cuba than I do because we experienced different "Cubas"—even though on paper (or in a pie graph) we are both counted as Cubans.

South Africa is another example of how two people could check the same box and yet have vastly different DQs. The actor Charlize Theron is South African and was born in 1976 during apartheid. A Black South African born in 1994 (the year apartheid ended) could arguably check the same box as Charlize Theron. They likely have different DQs around numerous things, including their African identity, apartheid, and more. Additionally, Charlize may have a significantly more diverse view regarding the wrongs of apartheid than an African-American born in Memphis.

You can take a look at any number of cities in the United States to understand how two people from the same place can look at a policy differently. In New York City, the policy of "stop-and-frisk" was a hot-button issue, and in recent years the NYPD has abandoned the controversial approach. Imagine a New Yorker of mixed Latino race, born and raised in Spanish Harlem, Brooklyn, or the Bronx who may have been victimized under "Stop & Frisk." He would totally understand what happened during that time produced a disproportionate impact on minorities. He would understand how the police can turn people against authority by overstepping their boundaries. Now imagine another New Yorker, a person of mixed Latino race who was born in Bermuda and settled in the Upper West Side because of his work in the Financial District. This person may support the intent of the law and oblivious to how it was enforced and applied. Hence, two New Yorkers can very much look alike on the outside, yet they may have very diverse views of the stop-and-frisk policy. These two people may know what stop-and-frisk is on the surface, but one has a high DQ with regard to the policy and the other does not.

The same can be said inside a company or organization. In order to ensure that policies, plans, and procedures don't have a negative impact on people within your organization (or your customers), you must have team members with varying DQs across a wide variety of topics that correlate to your company's product or services. Let's turn our focus to that now.

TRUE DIVERSITY *AT WORK*

I have developed these theories and principles as a result of my firsthand experiences in the workplace. The vast majority of my work experience is in the pharmaceutical industry, which I believe is a great case study. In pharmaceuticals, you develop a product for a particular patient/consumer that you then have to market and sell to that individual. More importantly, pharmaceuticals are specifically manufactured for a target customer base as defined by clinical data and the FDA-approved labeling. Therefore, understanding that customer base is critical to the success of the product and the company overall.

The importance of understanding the dynamics and cultural norms of a community/customer base became apparent to me on the basketball courts of Memorial Park. We didn't have a lot of crime in the area, but it was still pretty tough. You had to have street smarts, and you had to get along with everyone. It didn't matter whether they were Black, Puerto Rican, Cuban, Columbian, African American, Italian, Polish, German, or whatever— you had to learn how to get along with everyone. The more people you knew, the safer you were. Let me repeat that. The more people you knew and who knew you, the safer you were.

Let me illustrate this statement with a story from my childhood. We were playing a game of '21' with my basketball. My curfew was 6 p.m., but the game was still going on. I knew I couldn't just take my ball and leave because I would be toast on the playground from that moment forward. I also knew that my father didn't tolerate me being late, so I tried to find a compromise. I told them that I had to leave, but I would let them finish the game as long as they returned the ball to me the next day. The guys on the court remembered me as a kid that let them finish their game. I'd built their trust, and therefore I was able to connect to them on a different level. Believe me, had I tried to take the ball away to go home and leave them without a ball, I may have gotten the crap beaten out of me, and my life at the park would have been totally different from that point forward.

Question for you: Has someone at work taken the ball away and left you hanging on an important project or assignment? If you have experienced this, you know what I mean, especially if it was done for internal political motives.

Building the trust of the community is paramount to a company's success, and I learned that early on in my career. I graduated from pharmacy school in 1984 and started working that year for Schering-Plough as a sales rep. In less than two years, I became the youngest sales manager in the company's history. I was then recruited by the Southern

Regional Director, Ken Korte (one of the finest gentlemen ever to work in pharma). Something was going wrong in the Miami district, which went from Miami up to Palm Beach across to Naples, Florida. At the time, the area was growing tremendously in terms of population, but the district ranked last in the nation (50 out of 50) for growth in sales. Ken knew the company's approach needed to be analyzed and adjusted.

It was important to Ken that whoever replaced the manager would be able to get a deeper understanding of what was actually happening in Dade County, and Miami in particular. The reason for this was that Miami was the volume driver for the district. In order to generate the type of understanding the company needed, the manager had to be able to penetrate a mostly Cuban community. And for Ken, it wasn't enough that the person be bilingual; he knew that the new manager would need to understand the culture and build trust within the community. Ken chose me to take over a failing district and manage the area despite only being at Schering-Plough for two years. This was absolutely unheard of in the pharmaceutical industry and still remains an anomaly today.

I asked Ken why he had chosen such a young manager for such an important region. He told me that since I'd posted incredible sales numbers in Newark, New Jersey (which, like Miami, had previously been grossly under-performing), he was hoping that I could perform the same kind of turnaround in Florida. Ken said to me, "We believe that you have the street smarts, cultural background, and drive to get the job done." Ken knew of my Cuban heritage, and he also realized that like many of the doctors in the Miami area, my family fled Cuba to the United States. Ken believed that my upbringing would allow me to relate to the traditional and conservative Cuban population in Miami.

Ken was correct. I was able to gain the trust of the community in a relatively short period of time. I was able to build meaningful relationships, and the resulting conversations helped the company understand what the situation was, what we were doing correctly, what we were not doing, what the competition was doing, and so on. Ultimately, we had to let some people go for violations of our Code of Conduct, sloppy record keeping and poor customer relations. We also had closed some accounts that on the surface seemed to be very big accounts, but were actually detrimental to the company's reputation and position as a whole throughout the community.

Over the course of four years, we turned the district around and improved performance to the point that we won the President's Club award and had multiple people from the district promoted to higher positions within the company. Although I was not aware of it at the time, it all started by using the principles of TRUE DIVERSITY. My Diversity Quotient (DQ) allowed me to gain a thorough understanding of what was happening in the local medical community. It allowed for the creation of a safe environment where our customers told me the "Truth" and not the line that was being fed back to previous management. The only way to get to the truth was through building trusting relationships. The trust came from the willingness and ability to relate to the mindset and culture of the local medical community. By taking the time to truly understand "them," I was able to gain introductions to key decision-makers and influencers in the community. This step is instrumental in building true business relationships and using them as your edge. (If you have not already read Jerry Acuff's book, "The Relationship Edge in Business," you should.)

I was fortunate that Ken Korte understood the value of relationships in the selling process. He also understood that you do not build true relationships by counting the number of "details" made in a day. (Note: The term "details" is the name used in Pharma for a sales call. It's a horrible name, and that is exactly how our customers felt after a sales representative left an office—detailed). Instead, you build relationships by working hard to:

1. Understand your customer's issues,
   concerns, needs, wants, and desires

2. Deliver on promises made

By focusing on these two key points, you gain trust and build relationships that ultimately help you reach your business goals.

Once that trusting relationship is built, you begin to really sell. "Sales is essentially a transfer of feeling," Zig Ziglar has been quoted as saying. When the relationship has been cultivated, there is harmony between the intellectual and emotional components of the sales call. When businesses see the opportunity to understand and leverage the DQ of your sales staff, you are able to build relationships that are more resistant to competitive threats. Perhaps, that is what led Zig to also say, "Everything being equal, customers buy from people they like. Things being unequal, they still buy from people they like."

Later in my career, the need for a TRUE DIVERSITY approach to a problem was even better illustrated in the area of organ transplantation, specifically kidney transplants. My company was approaching a forecasting question strictly from a scientific and mathematical perspective. The market, as the company determined, was people who need kidney transplants. The company's forecasting logic was that at that time, there were approximately 14,000 kidney transplants a year. Roughly 80% of the organs came from deceased donors and only 20% from living donors. The need for kidney transplants clearly exceeded the number of organs donated per year. Pretty simple and straightforward— yet it failed to account for the characteristics of the communities that required transplants in the first place.

When you approach a problem from a TRUE DIVERSITY approach, you first must examine the community's pattern, customs, beliefs, and culture to determine what the problem is. From that approach, we discovered that the fastest-growing races that needed kidneys were African-Americans, Hispanics, and Hindis that had become westernized in many of their habits. These also happen to be populations that have not embraced the concept of organ donation.

Let's look at the Hindi population. Due to westernization, the Hindi community was beginning to develop higher rates of hypertension, diabetes, heart disease, and renal failure. Despite being one of the fastest-growing populations in need of kidney transplants, the Hindi population was also at the bottom for kidney donations. A traditional approach commonly used by Pharma was to build a donor awareness program to get more people signed up to be donors. This traditional program would ultimately be a waste of time and money. Guess what happens to the numbers of kidneys donated in the communities most in need of kidney transplants? It stays the same. Why? Because you did not understand the real issues blocking them from becoming donors.

A TRUE DIVERSITY approach, on the other hand, would start to engage and involve the leadership from the Hindi and African-American communities. It would change the dialogue. As you can see, I did not use the word "messaging." It is only through dialogue that you can actually change values and beliefs. You see, traditional Pharma approaches were aimed at the behaviors of these communities (e.g., they are not donating organs), whereas a TRUE DIVERSITY approach is aimed at understanding the values and beliefs that *drive* the behaviors. By changing the conversations around those beliefs, you begin to see changes in behaviors (e.g., an increase in the number of donated organs from those populations). For example, for some Hindis and Hispanics, there may be religious beliefs that prevent them from seeking medical care and/or donating organs, and this has to be considered when you are addressing the issue of organ donation. You also have to understand the deep distrust from some minority communities towards drug companies and the medical profession as a whole. Within the African-American community, there is a long-standing aversion towards participation in clinical trials and a distrust of doctors and hospitals because, at some points in the history of America, African-Americans were misled into serving as human subjects. Unless you understand the culture and beliefs of the community you're targeting, as well as their relationship to your product or service, you will fail to attract them. Lacking this understanding will render your efforts to change behavior as useless.

With regard to kidney transplantation, we worked with the Coalition of Black Churches to develop an educational campaign to dismiss negative myths about organ transplants. The campaign had to dispel any fears that the organs donated would be used for other purposes, and the church had to make it explicit that it was not against organ donations. We had to educate the community about the incredible need within their community, and we also had to inform them that diseases such as hypertension and diabetes increased the risk or renal failure and the need for a kidney transplant. Additionally, they were not aware of the number of African Americans that die while waiting for a kidney, nor were they aware of the shortage of donors from their communities. They had the ability to save lives within their very own community, and we would not have been able to reach them if we did not try to understand them. And we certainly would not have been able to understand the communities if we didn't have a truly diverse team targeting the issue.

IMPLEMENTING A **TRUE DIVERSITY** APPROACH

People often ask me about the timing of implementing a D&I strategy that encompasses the TRUE DIVERSITY principles. Businesses are set up to generate profit, and the hiring process in itself is a tedious task that often takes employees outside of Human Resources away from their primary function. Establishing a hiring process with an effective diversity strategy adds to that time. Now, I am encouraging people to take it a step further to ensure a truly diverse workforce. This will undoubtedly add time and effort to the process, but it is what is needed to actually realize the benefits of a diverse organization. Adding time to an already long interview process to ensure diversity of people, thought and experiences is certainly not an easy sale to executives and management. It is, however, necessary in today's competitive workforce and competitive global market.

A quote from Dr. Martin Luther King, Jr. comes to mind: "This is not the time to engage in the luxury of cooling off or to take the tranquilizing drug of gradualism." If we look back at the past fifty years, we have taken the gradual approach to D&I. The focus has been on the pie graph. Is this year's pie graph looking a little better than last year? Is this slice a bit bigger than it was last year? In so many cases, companies have accepted mediocre or slow growth in their D&I progress whereas they would not accept the same pace of growth in other areas of their business. Some executives look at D&I in terms of its burden on the company and not its benefit. Therefore, companies lack passionate and clear D&I strategies that promote substantial progress in the diversity of their workforce—or, more importantly, how the diversity of the organization improves their bottom-line.

My argument for TRUE DIVERSITY is that we need a more comprehensive approach to diversity that is based on change. The world is changing at warp speed thanks to the Internet, social media, and other forms of digital communication. Technology is forcing companies to understand that their client base is more diverse now and will continue to become more diverse in the years to come. Even if the customers "look the same" from the outside, their values and beliefs could be very different and the ability to measure those differences will help companies be successful in the digital world. More broadly, in order to continue to compete and grow in the global economy, companies have to match (or at least try to match) that speed of growth as it pertains to the diversity of the workforce. Just as companies are starting to embrace the fact that there is heterogenicity, socio-political and socio-economic factors and additional layers of complexity to the heterogenicity of customers.

Don't get me wrong; many companies are well aware of the growth trends impacting their customers within the global economy. Yet, they have failed to develop effective strategies that create a truly diverse workforce. An example that I saw firsthand was a company that needed to triple the size of its sales force to achieve the product's potential. To the company's credit, there was an initial focus on diversity in the hiring process. They started by casting a wide net, and when you looked at the pool of candidates, it appeared to be diverse.

The real questions should have been: "Who was actually getting hired from the pool of candidates, and for what positions?" A tug-of-war ensued because the hiring team was tasked with hiring a certain number of female and minority candidates by a deadline. On the surface, it appeared to be a noble goal (whatever you think about quotas). However, these self-imposed timelines drive a conflict between hiring a truly diverse workforce and meeting hiring timelines. Sure enough, although they started with a diverse pool of candidates, the end result did not improve the diversity of the sales force. To make matters worse, I am certain that hiring managers were rewarded for meeting the hiring timelines, further communicating that "diversity" is not as important as hiring fast. A "hiring fast" approach is generally an incorrect strategy in business.

Let's take a little deeper look at this situation. The company merely sought to replicate the diversity numbers they had previously, but this time on a much larger scale. Management evaluated the performance and in essence communicated, "The diversity make-up of the salesforce post-expansion mirrored the pre-expansion so we're doing well." A closer look revealed something far more important about the group of new hires, however. The diversity numbers did mimic the overall population of the entire company, but in this case, the majority of the minorities that were new hires were hired for lower-level or entry-jobs. There was very little improvement in management and none at all in executive sales positions.

Interesting to note that the customer base for the company's product was highly diverse, and the way to market and sell to that customer base required a broad approach and understanding of the various market players. Ultimately, the product did not perform, as it should have. The company may have understood the demographics of the overall customer base, but they did not have a team in place (particularly in decision-making positions) that truly understood: 1) the unique benefits of the product; 2) which patients really needed the product; 3) why they needed it more than the general customer base; and, 4) how to access those patients and their support systems. Had the company taken an approach that favored TRUE DIVERSITY, I believe it would have fared far better in the marketplace.

As this example demonstrates, it is imperative that a TRUE DIVERSITY approach starts at the most senior levels of leadership. I would have advised a strategy that flowed from the C-Suite down to the senior managers. If the direction to hire a diverse sales team came from the highest level of the organization, not only would more minorities and women have been hired, they would have been hired into decision-making and management positions. It also signals a company-wide strategy that is about more than numbers and quotas. It is a strategy that is committed to TRUE DIVERSITY.

The commitment has to extend beyond the hiring process. There has to be a corporate culture that not only allows and encourages employees to contribute diverse ideas but also celebrates those contributions. If the company in our example had: 1) hired diverse employees into management and key roles, and 2) empowered those employees to participate in the marketing and strategy development for the communities they represented, then they would have been far more successful in the launch of the product.

One company that I see getting it right is Johnson & Johnson ("J&J"). In its credo, the company makes it clear that diversity is a "must" and employees "must" feel free to communicate their ideas. Here is the section of their credo that spells it out:

> We are responsible to our employees who work with us throughout the world. We *must* provide an inclusive work environment where each person *must* be considered as an individual. We *must* respect their diversity and dignity and recognize their merit. They *must* have a sense of security, fulfillment and purpose in their jobs. Compensation *must* be fair and adequate and working conditions clean, orderly and safe. We must support the health and well-being of our employees and help them fulfill their family and other personal responsibilities. Employees *must* feel free to make suggestions and complaints. There *must* be equal opportunity for employment, development and advancement for those qualified. We *must* provide highly capable leaders and their actions must be just and ethical.[8] (Emphasis added).

> J&J's D&I statement expands on the statements in the credo: Diversity at Johnson & Johnson is about your unique perspective. It's about you, your colleagues and the world we care for—all backgrounds, beliefs and the entire range of human experience—coming together. You view the world from a unique vantage point; a perspective that gives you problem-solving potential ideas, solutions & strategies that, when mobilized, can bring health to billions.

* * *

Be yourself, change the world.

Our vision at Johnson & Johnson is for every person to use their unique experiences and backgrounds, together – to spark solutions that create a better, healthier world.

* * *

Make diversity and inclusion how we work every day.

Our mission is to make diversity & inclusion our way of doing business. We will advance our culture of belonging where open hearts and minds combine to unleash the potential of the brilliant mix of people, in every corner of Johnson & Johnson.[9]

Words matter, and the emphasis that the J&J credo puts on the word "must" underscores the company's commitment to D&I. There is no room for interpretation. The use of the word "must" set forth a company-wide mandate that is echoed in its D&I statement. It doesn't say we "strive to" or "our goal is to" provide an inclusive work environment. No, it states, "We *must* provide an inclusive work environment where each person *must* be considered as an individual."

While words matter, actions matter most. I've studied J&J, and I can attest that they put their words into action. The company is constantly living up to its credo and D&I commitment, which is clearly found in the following statements by their CEO, Alex Gorsky:

"As Chairman and CEO of Johnson & Johnson and Chair of the Business Roundtable Corporate Governance Committee, I've witnessed how a commitment to diversity and inclusion has the power to positively transform a company and the lives of its employees. But this commitment and this transformation does not happen by accident, nor does it occur overnight. It takes a sustained focus by all of a company's employees—especially its leadership. It requires setting the tone at the top that diversity and inclusion is a strategic business imperative. It calls for a conscious dedication to identify the potential biases or barriers to opportunities within a company's internal processes. It demands continuous attention to improving those processes, removing barriers, developing a system of accountability and metrics, and reinforcing a culture of belonging where people of all backgrounds, beliefs, and experiences feel valued for their contributions.

"Advancing diversity and inclusion in corporate America depends on leadership at all levels. The companies that invest in diversity and inclusion today will be the most innovative, sustainable and prosperous tomorrow. By accepting this shared responsibility, together we can seize a tremendous shared opportunity to create a more vibrant US economy where all Americans can realize their potential."

TRUE DIVERSITY *IN ACTION*

First, I want to come straight out and challenge the practice of combining diversity and inclusion. To me, it's like when you take strawberry, vanilla, and chocolate ice cream and blend them together— you get a nasty-looking mush that is clearly dominated by the chocolate, regardless of how good the vanilla or strawberry might be. You do not get to evaluate the quality of any of them individually.

I think that by combining diversity and inclusion into one strategy, companies get a hodge-podge that lacks the individual focus that diversity and inclusion deserve independently. Many D&I efforts result in a more diverse organization, but they fail on the inclusion of that diverse workforce.

THE NEED TO EVALUATE "D & I" SEPERATLY

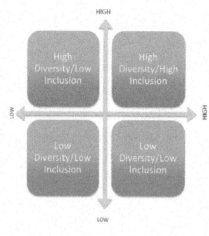

- Companies may appear to be diverse, but may not be very inclusive.

- Others may appear to be to less diverse but yet, very inclusive.

(Image 3.1)

DI: Measured Independently leads to 4 Segments

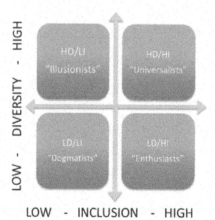

- Illusionists
  - Diverse for show? Or do they honestly not know how to be inclusive?
- Dogmatists
  - Surviving for now under their norms
- Enthusiasts
  - Like a wine enthusiast, likes the experience wants/needs more
- Universalists
  - They get it, externally focused

(Image 3.2)

Reality of the Four D&I QUADRANTS

- Very Few HD/HI "Universalist
  - Universalists make market noise not D&I noise
- Too many HD/LI and LD/LI
  - Make D&I noise and focus on efforts not results

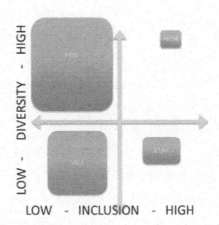

(Image 3.3)

Second, I want to challenge the convention of showing graphs as a marker of a company's successful diversity and inclusion strategy. A pie graph merely shows the numbers of people—usually segmented by gender and race—who work for the company. It is a two-dimensional tool that is intended to address a multi-dimensional issue. My hope is that this book and my principles force people to think way beyond that two-dimensional piece of paper and begin to think more deeply about diversity.

Third, my goal is to provide real-life examples of how and when TRUE DIVERSITY has played out in practice rather than in theory. In the following chapters, I will demonstrate how developing a diversity AND an inclusion strategy with the TRUE DIVERSITY approach will increase the bottom line, improve employee morale, and add to the overall success of a company. I have experienced this success from the front lines as a manager and then as an executive.

Finally, and this point is personal, I want people to strongly consider ageism in developing their diversity strategies. In the current job market, the new phrase for "you're too old" is "you're overqualified." I want to submit to Merriam-Webster that an alternative definition of "overqualified" is "too old." With so much emphasis placed on millennials and the digital generation, older employees have found it increasingly difficult to maintain employment, advance, or find employment once they become unemployed. In many instances, these ageist-hiring practices are in conflict with the demographics of a company's customers.

Taking the TRUE DIVERSITY approach and applying the principles in this book will prove to be a good investment for any company, regardless of size or industry. The goal is to better understand your employees so they are encouraged to help you better understand and market to your customers. The world is rapidly changing, and so too is your workforce. The way you approach hiring and including that workforce must change as well. Gradually growing to a truly diverse workforce is a thing of the past. Be active. Be aggressive. Be inclusive.

CHAPTER 2:

Diversity & the Bottomline

"**Companies that embrace diversity and inclusion in all aspects
of their business statistically outperform their peers.**"
—Josh Bersin

At this point, it is well-established and extensively researched that diversity and inclusion both have a direct impact on a company's bottom line. Two of the leading consulting companies, McKinsey & Company and Deloitte Consulting, recently conducted studies on diversity and inclusion in the workplace, and both had similar findings with regard to the positive effects a diverse workforce has not only on a company's bottom line profit, but also for the viability of the company overall.

In its study titled, "Why Diversity Matters," McKinsey makes the case for profit benefit right from the beginning. The McKinsey study reviewed the data for "366 public companies across a range of industries in Canada, Latin America, the United Kingdom, and the United States," and they found that "new research makes it *increasingly clear that companies with more diverse workforces perform better financially.*"[10] One of the key questions the study sought to answer was the likelihood that companies in the top quartile for diversity would outperform companies in the bottom quartile. McKinsey found that gender-diverse companies are fifteen percent more likely to outperform bottom-ranking companies.[11] There's even stronger evidence for companies that are ethnically diverse. Those companies are thirty-five percent more likely to outperform non-diverse companies in the lower quartile.[12] It goes without saying that those bottom-ranking companies are less likely to achieve above-average returns in comparison to national industry medians.

McKinsey further clarifies, "[w]hile correlation does not equal causation (greater gender and ethnic diversity in corporate leadership doesn't automatically translate into more profit), the correlation does indicate that when companies commit themselves to diverse leadership, they are more successful."[13] McKinsey acknowledges, however, that an analysis that looks only at a company's profits is not a full picture of success. Diverse companies also are able to better attract top talent, retain employees, and maintain overall employee satisfaction than companies that are not diverse. These intangible assets also strongly contribute to the company's overall success and, ultimately, its profit margin.

One of McKinsey's key statements supports many of the TRUE DIVERSITY premises set forth in this book. Race and gender are the traditional two-dimensional ways we look at diversity, and based on McKinsey's findings, both clearly play a role in propping up a company's balance sheet. However, the report suggests that other factors that approach diversity from a multi-dimensional vantage point also factor into a company's success. McKinsey concluded:

> This in turn suggests that other kinds of diversity – for example, in age, sexual orientation, and experience (*such as a global mindset and cultural fluency*) – are also likely to bring some level of competitive advantage for companies that can attract and retain such diverse talent. (emphasis added).[14]

The phrase "global mind-set and cultural fluency" is similar to what I have proposed around a person's DQ ("Diversity Quotient") in Chapter One. Going beyond race and gender in a diversity initiative is not only prudent; it is in direct relationship to putting a company in a position of advantage over its competition. It's not only the right thing to do—it is a best practice that will lead to improved market position.

Two additional findings from the McKinsey study are worth pointing out to further illustrate the positive effect a diverse workforce has on a company's financial performance:

- In the United States, there is a linear relationship between racial and ethnic diversity and better financial performance: for every 10 percent increase in racial and ethnic diversity on the senior executive team, earnings before interest and taxes (EBIT) rise 0.8 percent.

- In the United Kingdom, greater gender diversity on the senior-executive team corresponded to the highest performance uplift in our data set: for every 10 percent increase in gender diversity, EBIT rose by 3.5 percent.[15]

The last line of the report agrees with my argument against the gradualism approach that far too many companies have implemented. The time for TRUE DIVERSITY is now, and it is imperative for any company that wants to stay competitive. "Given the higher returns that diversity is expected to bring, we believe it is better to invest now, since winners will pull further ahead and laggards will fall further behind."[16]

Deloitte, in its study, 'The Diversity and Inclusion Revolution: Eight Powerful Truths," makes an even stronger case for a multi-dimensional, multi-pronged, and multi-level approach to diversity and inclusion. The first of the eight truths is that "diversity of thinking is the new frontier."[17] This parallels the concepts proposed regarding a person's DQ. Deloitte found that diversity of thinking yields creativity and enhances innovation by approximately twenty percent.[18] In addition, a team's ability to troubleshoot and predict risks goes up by thirty percent, and it also facilitates team buy-in and trust.[19]

———————————— FIGURE 1 | The value of diversity of thinking ————————————

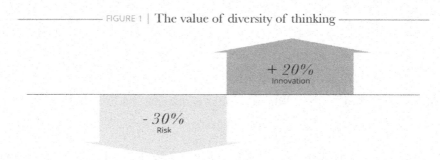

Source: Juliet Bourke, *Which Two Heads Are Better Than One? How Diverse Teams Create Breakthrough Ideas and Make Smarter Decisions* (Australian Institute of Company Directors, 2016).

Deloitte Insights | deloitte.com/insights

(Image 4)

Deloitte's research reveals that high-performing teams are both cognitively *and* demographically diverse. By cognitive diversity, [Deloitte is] referring to educational and functional diversity, as well as diversity in the mental frameworks that people use to solve problems. A complex problem typically requires input from six different mental frameworks or "approaches": evidence, options, outcomes, people, process, and risk. [omitted] Demographic diversity, for its part, helps teams tap into knowledge and networks specific to a particular demographic group.[20]

Deloitte's findings underscore the need for a TRUE DIVERSITY approach to a company's diversity and inclusion strategy. An employee's race and gender may provide insight into their thinking, but it's merely a starting point. To truly engender diversity of thinking, a diversity strategy needs to identify and explore an employee or an applicant's background in a way that ensures a holistic view of that person's available assets to the company or a specific team.

In hard numbers, Deloitte found that diversity of thinking increased innovation by twenty percent and decreased risk by thirty percent.[21] The other seven truths outlined in the study will be addressed at various points throughout this book. One worth noting now supports another assertion made in Chapter One: "Diversity without inclusion is not enough." As I stated, D&I are often lumped together even though they should be examined and explored separately. Without inclusion, the financial benefits of a truly diverse workforce are diminished or negated.

It goes beyond financial profits when discussing the benefits of diversity to a company's success. A company is only as good as its employees. An engaged, experienced, creative, and committed workforce breeds innovation, which ultimately enhances a company's position in the marketplace—as well as their profits. Being able to attract and retain top industry talent gives companies a competitive advantage over those that don't. The cost of hiring new talent increases by the year, so retaining that talent is not only advantageous, but it also saves money.

SHRM Human Capital Benchmarking studies have placed the cost per hire of a new employee anywhere from $2,500 to $4,000 depending on a company's size and industry.[22] Employment placement and headhunters typically charge fifteen to twenty percent of an employee's annual salary, and once you add the costs of training and other line items related to the hiring process, the cost for hiring a new employee weighs heavily on a company's balance sheets.

It is also well established that diversity leads to innovation. "While business lore tends to link innovation with a creative drive that is exclusive to the top and brightest talent, true innovation thrives in an inclusive culture that values diverse ideas, leverages unique perspectives and invites everyone to achieve collaborative breakthroughs across the entire organization," noted Donald Fan, Senior Director of Diversity at Walmart, in his 2011 study.[23]

Qantas Airlines is a great example of how a diverse workforce not only leads to innovation but can also save a company from corporate failure. The Australian airline was in dire straits in 2013 as a result of increased fuel prices, aircraft issues, and a prolonged union dispute. Within four years, Qantas was able to turn its position around and delivered record profits in 2017. It also won numerous industry awards (including "World's Safest Airline") while being ranked as Australia's most trusted big business. Qantas CEO, Alan Joyce, attributed the company's turnaround success directly to the diversity and inclusiveness of its workforce.

"We have a very diverse environment *and* a very inclusive culture," said Joyce.[24] The Qantas CEO continued to laud its diversity and inclusion efforts by saying: "[Our diverse and inclusive workforce] got us through the tough times"[25] and "diversity generated better strategy, better risk management, better debates, and better outcomes."[26] Joyce is not alone in his assertion. According to Deloitte's 2017 "Global Human Capital Trends" report, two-thirds of company leaders that were included in a 10,000-person survey cited diversity and inclusion as "important" or "very important" to business.[27]

Apple, Inc., one of the most innovative companies in history, is even more emphatic and unequivocal in its support of a diverse workforce. In Apple's own words, "The most innovative company must also be the most diverse. We take a holistic view of diversity that looks beyond usual measurements. A view that includes the varied perspectives of our employees as well as app developers, suppliers, and anyone who aspires to a future in tech. Because we know new ideas come from diverse ways of seeing things."[28]

Apple takes a TRUE DIVERSITY approach to its D&I strategy. It embraces and promotes the varied perspectives, backgrounds, and experiences of its employees because it knows that an employee's DQ is paramount to innovation. For a technology company like Apple, innovation is its bread and butter. If the Apple workforce is not generating innovative, groundbreaking ideas, it loses its competitive advantage and will ultimately lose market share in the ultra-competitive tech industry.

Even with all of the evidence that substantiates the well-settled fact that diversity positively impacts the bottom line, I think it's unwise for profit to be a company's sole impetus for pursuing a D&I strategy. For any company or executive who would assert that profit is the leading, if not singular, factor in developing and implementing a D&I strategy, I would say: "It's not about you (or the company, for that matter). It's about your customer."

First, if companies only focus on profit, it can skew the way they approach diversity. If you have a non-diverse group within a company that looks at their year-over-year performance, and they determine that they experienced growth, they will take pride and applaud themselves. Now, let's assume the growth they experienced was moderate, ranging from 6% to 8%—not bad a year-to-year in their industry. For that company, if profit growth is the only argument for diversity, it becomes a harder sale. Particularly, the company might feel no immediate need to diversify its workforce if the industry overall is not growing faster than 6%. They're celebrating growing above the industry average and see no need for change.

The problem is that no one is looking at the company's forecast using a diverse lens that could have provided superior growth above what they had experienced. (This is what David Foster meant when he said, "The enemy of great is good.") If our hypothetical company had looked at growth through a diverse lens, it may have been looking for exponential growth. The studies are clear that diversity impacts growth at significant positive percentages, so instead of the moderate growth, it could have grown at 20% or more. And to that company, I say that if you don't look at the potential diversity can have on your company, you're merely complacent with the average—which means you're not doing your best business.

My second reason for encouraging companies to go beyond profit growth in seeking to implement a diversity strategy is that many of the factors that are impacted by diversity are never measured. These factors—such as company culture, employee satisfaction, and retention rates—are not typically measured on a balance sheet. But as clearly evidenced in the aforementioned studies, these are factors that have a direct relationship with the company's overall success. If you say those words ("company culture") to many of the old-guard managers or executives, you may get laughed out of the room. But every executive understands (or should understand) the other factors like innovation and creativity, which are not measured on a profit-and-loss statement even though the impact can't be denied.

In Marcus Buckingham and Curt Coffman's book, "First, Break All the Rules: What the World's Greatest Managers Do Differently," the authors offer solutions to improve employee satisfaction using examples from the best managers in business. As the title suggests, the authors state that in order for a company to succeed beyond its linear growth, it must first break all of the rules that it has previously followed. The same is true about how diversity is measured.

In an ideal world, a company could set up a marketing experiment between two teams—one non-diverse team and the other a truly diverse team (in thinking, background, age, etc.). If a company is faced with a challenge or market opportunity, they should bring in two teams with as equal qualifications as possible. Then, they should task the teams to solve market issues. Did the range of opportunities or solutions increase in the diverse group or not? Did the understanding of the opportunities increase or not?

When looking at possible applications of the solutions, companies must measure the ability to execute the solutions of the non-diverse group against those of the diverse group. My bet is that the range of executable applications for the diverse team will be significantly larger than the non-diverse team. But as we know, companies don't measure it that way. Why not? Perhaps because it would increase expenses or add some time to the analysis. Or perhaps they might be afraid of proving that there is a better way than what that they have been doing for a long time. Or simply because they don't want to accept the results if they did measure it this way. Hence, my assertion is that companies need to break the rules in the way they measure (or experiment) with diversity. Simply put, you can't get the best solution if the potential source of the solution is not in the room.

This brings me back to my point that it's not about the company; it's about the customer. There are three things a company should look at to inform its diversity strategy. First, in terms of diversity, looking at a company's customer or client base is far more important than looking at the P&L sheet. (Of course, the P&L is where a business review starts and ends. My point is that you won't experience the positive impact that a TRULY DIVERSE team can have on a P&L if you do not become TRULY DIVERSE). Talk to your customers—your client base will tell you everything you need to know. Go a step further and survey your customers. See what your customers think, need, and want from your product (or similar products). Secondly, look at the recruitment and HR policies of your current competition and ask some key questions. Are the recruitment practices of your competitors landing the higher potential minority candidates? Are more and higher potential minorities being referred to your competitors? Do your competitors have more advanced mentoring programs for minorities? Finally, and I think most companies do not do this, do a forward-thinking analysis of your industry, your product, and your competition from your customer's point of view. Where do they think your business will be in five or ten years? How does their view compare to your vision of your future business? If it looks different, it is time to start worrying. More importantly, it is time to start changing by incorporating a more diverse and customer-centric solution to your challenges. When the likes of Honda, Toyota, and Datsun first hit the automobile market, consumers were looking for reliable, gas-efficient, four-cylinder cars. Yet US carmakers kept pumping out eight-cylinder gas-guzzlers. This allowed Japanese carmakers to create an entirely new category of low-cost, fuel-efficient, low-frills automobiles. All Chevy, Ford, and Chrysler had to do was to listen to the public and they would have been able to introduce a decent four-cylinder car and not give up such a huge part of the market.

THE CURSE OF KNOWLEDGE

One of my favorite topics is a phenomenon called the curse of knowledge. The term "curse of knowledge" was developed and first used by Colin Camerer, George Loewenstein and Martin Weber—all economists—in a 1989 *Journal of Political Economy* article.[29] According to Jane Kennedy, "The curse of knowledge is a cognitive bias that occurs when an individual, communicating with other individuals, unknowingly assumes that the others have the background to understand."[30]

In his book, "Made to Stick: Why Some Ideas Survive and Others Die," Chip Heath gives an example of an experiment using a group of college students. One group of students was given a list of popular songs and was instructed to tap out the melody and rhythm with their fingers. The other group of students were placed behind a partition and were instructed to identify the list of songs based on the finger tapping. The researchers asked the tapping students what percentage of the songs they thought the hidden students would get correct. On average, the tapping students believed that the hidden students would get 50% or more of the songs correct.

The curse of knowledge comes into play because the tapping students believed what they were tapping matched the song. In reality, what they were actually tapping sounded nothing like the songs to the hidden students. In almost every instance, the hidden students guessed between 2-3% of the songs correctly. It undermined what the tapping students believed to be an accurate reflection of the songs they were given.

The reason why it's important in this matter is because the curse of knowledge happens all too often in companies, particularly when it comes to diversity. Let's say you have a CEO giving a big company-wide speech. These speeches are known for their exuberant platitudes like:

- "We're going to be number one in customer service;"
- "We're going to make our customers happy;" or,
- "We're going to be the most innovative company."

The CEO thinks that the employees listening to the message clearly understand what it takes to be number one in customer satisfaction or the most innovative company. I'm pretty sure General Motors and Ford suffered from this a while back when they were being outperformed by Japanese automakers. I'm also pretty sure this type of thinking led to the creation of the hideous Pontiac Aztek. The Aztek is the perfect example of what happens with the curse of knowledge when the speaker assumes that an unclear message is in fact clear.

I apply the same concept to a term I call the "curse of non-diverse knowledge."

Below is the original concept by Jane Kennedy.

The Curse of Knowledge

• The Curse of - Knowledge:

- is a cognitive bias that occurs when an individual, communicating with other individuals, unknowingly assumes that the others have the background to understand[1]

- is a cognitive bias that knowing the outcome of a certain event makes it seem more predictable than may actually be true[2]

- (1)Kennedy, Jane (1995). "Debiasing the Curse of Knowledge in Audit Judgment". *The Accounting Review.* **70** (2): 249–273. JSTOR 248305
- (2)Camerer, Colin; Loewenstein, George; Weber, Martin (1989). "The Curse of Knowledge in Economic Settings: An Experimental Analysis" (PDF). *Journal of Political Economy.* **97** (5): 1232–1254. doi:10.1086/261651

(Image 5.1)

Here is an explanation of my adaptation.

The Curse of Non-Diverse Knowledge

A homogenous group of smart co-workers tend to see the world through a similar lens. Groups normally align on the best "accepted" solution which unintentionally chokes off innovation outside their agreed upon, narrow view.

 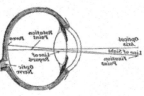 

When The Curse of Knowledge's cognitive bias is superimposed on a homogenous, smart group of people – the result is a narrow view of:
- Their customers need
- Solutions preferred by their customers
- Possible risks, threats and opportunities

(Image 5.2)

Removing The Curse of Non-Diverse Knowledge

A heterogenous group of smart co-workers apply different lenses resulting in a broader view and not choking off innovation so readily.

 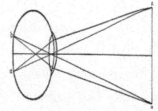 

The Curse of Knowledge's cognitive bias may be minimized by a increasing the heterogenicity of a group. Why?
- Increased challenges to individual cognitive bias
- Broader view of:
  - customer needs
  - solutions preferred by their customers
  - possible risks, threats and opportunities

(Image 5.3)

Basically, the curse of non-diverse knowledge starts when you have a homogenous group of people who tend to see the world through a similar lens. These groups normally align on the best-accepted solutions, which unintentionally chokes off innovation outside their agreed-upon but ultimately narrow view. In the preceding figures, you have all of the members of the homogenous group giving their opinions and raising their hands—they all look the same, and they see the world through a narrow lens that reflects a limited, similar worldview. When the curse of knowledge's cognitive bias is superimposed on a homogenous group of people, the result is a *narrow* view of 1) what their customers need; 2) what solutions their customers would prefer; 3) possible opportunities; and, 4) possible risks and threats.

If you remove the curse of non-diverse knowledge (which can only be done by adding diversity and inclusion), you have a heterogeneous group of co-workers who apply different lenses resulting in a broader view that does not cut off access to innovation (**see Images 5.1-5.3**). In this case, the Curse of Knowledge's cognitive bias may be minimized by increasing the heterogeneity of a group because the result is a *broader* view of 1) what their customers need; 2) what solutions their customers would prefer; 3) possible opportunities; and, 4) possible risks and threats.

A personal example that best illustrates this is when I was in the market for an SUV for my family back in the 1990s. The SUV was primarily for my wife to transport my daughters and their friends to school and various activities. The two mammoth trucks available at the time were the Chevy Suburban and the Ford Expedition. In 1992, GM dropped the height of the running board on the Suburban by 3.2 inches because most of the people driving the truck were women. I don't know this for certain, but I would bet that a diverse group realized that women with families were their customer base, and so they changed the design to account for that fact. Ultimately, we purchased the Suburban because "it was easier to get in and out of" for my wife and family.

The financial case for diversity should be well-settled by now. Unlike so many other corporate and workplace issues, there really isn't much debate amongst the experts in the field that a diverse workforce leads to increased profits and performance. The TRUE DIVERSITY approach, however, encourages companies to go beyond the balance sheet and think about the customers and clients. In my view, it is a far more appropriate and accurate basis for a company's decision to diversify its workforce. The world is diverse, and so too are your customers. Any company that isn't moving toward a progressive—and, I would emphasize, an aggressive—approach to diversity will find themselves left behind in this ever-increasing global economy.

CHAPTER 3:

True Diversity & Innovation

**"If you change the way you look at things,
the things you look at change." —Wayne Dyer**

In 2019, Global consulting company Accenture published a full-report titled *Equality = Innovation. Getting to Equal 2019: Creating a culture that drives innovation,* which makes the case for companies to create diverse cultures that will not only drive innovation, but will be prepared for the rapidly changing global economy. According to the study's authors, "Innovation equals survival. It's well documented that in this age of widespread disruption, companies must innovate continuously, creating new markets, experiences, products, services content or process."[31] As I have said, the old days of gradualism won't work. Companies must adopt an aggressive diversity strategy now; if not, they are writing the company's obituary. The Accenture study goes on to argue:

> Nearly everyone wants—and needs—to innovate. Ninety-
> five percent of business leaders see innovation as vital to
> competitiveness and business viability, and 91 percent
> of employees want to be innovative. But while 76 percent

of leaders say they regularly empower employees to be innovative, only 42 percent of employees agree.[32]

Before we proceed with this discussion, it is helpful to review some of the key studies surrounding diversity and innovation. *The Mix of Talent Matters* by The Boston Consulting Group ("BCG") and the Technological University of Munich looked at 171 European companies in Germany, Switzerland, and Austria, with one-third having over 10,000 employees and one-third having less than 1,000 employees. Because it is difficult to empirically prove the link between diversity in management to innovation, BCG & TUM applied some mathematical and statistical methods "to quantify the impact that different types of diversity have on companies' ability to generate new sources of revenue."[33] The study definitively showed that there is a direct link between diversity and innovation.

Overall, the study found four insights that I found significant. The first was there was clearly a positive relationship between management diversity and innovation. Secondly, the study found that the innovation boost was not relegated to a single type of diversity. Diversity in industry background, country of origin, career path, and gender were the four types of diversity that boosted innovation. It also went further to say that for a multi-dimensionally diverse person (e.g., female and Black with a diverse industry background), innovation increased for every additional variable. The third insight they found is that the improvements in innovation were particularly positive in the larger companies and had a greater impact as the organizations became more complex. The fourth insight they discovered was that gender diversity needs to "go beyond tokenism," meaning that gender diversity affects innovation only at significant levels (more than 20%) in management positions. Finally, the study found that the diverse management teams that fostered input from lower-level workers where employees felt free to speak their minds were also critical to sparking innovation.[34]

Back to the bottom line. The BCG study found that more diverse companies generated 38% more revenue from new products and services (the indicators used to quantify innovation revenue) in the three years preceding the study than companies that were less diverse. Companies with the greatest gender diversity generated 34% more innovation revenue compared to 25% innovation revenue generated by companies with less gender diversity (e.g., where only 1 in 20 managers were female).[35] The authors stated that "the evidence also suggests that having a high percentage of female managers is positively correlated with disruptive innovation, in which a new product, service or business model fully replaces the version that existed before (such as what Netflix has done to DVD rental stores and what Amazon is doing to retail)."[36]

Not surprisingly, the study also found that in terms of diversity in age, companies needed to do some work across the board. According to BCG, companies haven't learned how to appropriately integrate different levels of seniority of their workforce. "Cross-generational intelligence" needs to account for the divergent expectations in which generations of employees, particularly in management positions, work. I believe this should be a focus for companies that wish to utilize and leverage the assets across the generational gaps of its employees. More senior leaders bring a wealth of knowledge, experience, and historical information that will aid less-senior leaders who bring fresh ideas, a younger perspective, and new energy. Collectively, these diverse leaders in terms of age compliment a company's innovation by ensuring a global approach to challenges that includes experience and inspiration. Moreover, in the pharmaceutical industry a senior leader may have significantly more in common with their customer base. This is especially true in diseases like heart failure, chronic obstructive pulmonary disease (COPD), Type II diabetes, osteoporosis, most cancers, *etc.* To reflect the customer/patient base, pharmaceutical companies should include older employees in senior management roles and decision making.

The BCG study also states that a company must go beyond a "numbers game" to foster innovation through diversity. In order for diversity to foster innovation, the study found that five conditions need to present in the workplace:

- **Participative Leadership Behavior.** When managers genuinely listen to employees' suggestions and make use of them, diversity's benefits multiply.

- **Openness to Cognitive Diversity.** This describes a dynamic in which employees feel free to speak their minds.

- **Strategic Priority.** At some companies, diversity has considerable top management support.

- **Frequent Interpersonal Communication.** When companies find ways to facilitate dialogue between people with different backgrounds, it can provide a creative spark and bolster innovation.

- **Equal Employment Practices.** Many companies still don't have equitable employment, either in policy or practice.[37]

Companies that have favorable work environments generate over a third of their revenue from innovation, while companies that don't have favorable work environments generate less than a quarter of revenue from innovation. Profit margins at diverse companies with favorable work environments are higher. All in all, the BCG study concluded that management diversity boosts innovation. This moves the question from "whether' to 'what now?' And that's when progress begins."[38]

The next study I want to examine is one highlighted by Fast Company, the editorial publication and business devoted to business innovation. The article summarizing the study, "Want A More Innovative Company? Simple: Hire A More Diverse Workforce," points to the research conducted by North Carolina State professor Richard Warr.[39] Professor Warr and his team of researchers looked at 3,000 publicly traded company from 2001 to 2014. The top finding of the research was that diverse companies were significantly more innovative than non-diverse companies. Even more interesting to me was the fact that diverse companies were far more resilient during the 2008 financial crisis.

The study looked across nine measures of diversity, including the diversity of C-suite leadership, promotion rates for women and people of color to "profit and loss responsibilities," as well as the companies' policies for its LGBTQ and disabled employees.[40] Companies that had positive indicators around all nine of the diversity measures announced, on average, two extra products per year, which was double the average for major companies with lower indicators (or that did not fulfill all nine measures).

Professor Warr believes that there are three main reasons why more diverse companies are better innovators. First, diverse teams present a broader range of perspectives, interests, experiences, and backgrounds from which to problem-solve and innovate. Therefore, the knowledge of the customer base is wider and deeper. These diverse teams think about problems differently than non-diverse teams. The second factor is that diverse companies attract diverse talent. People from diverse backgrounds gravitate to companies where they see themselves represented versus companies where they'd be a token member of the team. Finally, Warr asserts that more diverse companies gain a "halo effect" in that they're more attractive to women and minorities, but also to people who believe in and celebrate diversity as an asset.

It should be apparent that diverse teams generate diverse ideas. Unfortunately, this is not always the case. Once again, it's about the customer and not diversity for diversity's sake. Many industries talk about "the customer journey." The customer journey is simply a recording of all of the steps a customer takes to acquire your product or service. The problem with relying on a homogenous team to record a customer journey is that they will all tend to see and subsequently report similar journeys. A diverse team has a higher likelihood of seeing things differently so what they record could be quite different. For example, a set of instructions for a new product that can only be found on the web may not be flagged as an issue by 5 non-minority marketers from a prosperous neighborhood(they have internet access on their phones, tablets, computers) , but could be flagged as a problem by someone that lives in the mountains of West Virginia or someone without an internet access on mobile devices. "As you evolve a product or development team to include people with different perspectives and experiences, you enhance your ability to better understand the needs of your current and potential customers."[41]

According to a 2018 Forbes article, Facebook provided a perfect example this. The social media and tech company adopted a "real name" policy for its users that ultimately failed because it didn't consider the diversity of its user base. Facebook developed technology and software that sought to weed out fake profile names from actual users' real names. It did not take into account the extreme diversity of its user population and their actual names. The technology Facebook developed was incapable of recognizing non-Anglo-Saxon names, "for example, Shane Creepingbear and Dana Lone Hill, both Native American names."[42] It is highly likely that the homogeneity of Facebook's technology development team led to this significant misstep and miscalculation, which ultimately upset many of its users.

The 2019 Accenture report discussed earlier is the most direct in its findings and recommendations. "Accenture has found that a culture of equality—the same kind of workplace environment that helps everyone advance to higher positions—is a powerful multiplier of innovation and growth."[43] Simply put, if a company wants to innovate, it must be a company of equality. Companies that have equal work cultures are six times more likely to innovate than companies that are not as equal.[44] The global consulting company calculates that the global GDP would "increase by up to US$8 trillion by 2028 if innovation mindset in all countries were raised by ten percent."[45] The report goes on to show the direct correlation between an equal company culture and innovation. A 10% improvement in the cultural factors identified in the report translates to a 10.6% increase in innovation mindset.

Mastercard is often hailed as one of the examples of a company that has an equality culture and uses it to advance innovation. According to Ajay Banga, President and CEO of Mastercard,

> "We're in an industry where technology and innovation flow around you all the time. If you surround yourself with people who look like you, walk like you, talk like you, went to the same schools as you and had the same experiences, you'll have the very same blind spots. You'll miss the same trends, curves in the road and opportunities."[46]

It's not just lip service, either. Mastercard has twice the number of women in leadership positions than the great majority of other companies in the S&P 500. "Diversity is built into the core of what we do," says Banga, and it would appear that he means it.

Accenture also found that an equal culture can inspire innovation across all industries, countries, and workforce demographics. An equal culture also has a positive effect on employees from the varied diversity measures—gender, race, background, sexual orientation, age, and ethnicity. In summation, Accenture found that "[a]gainst every factor we tested, culture wins" and leads to innovation.

Having to ask whether diversity leads to innovation is behind the times. Of course, diversity leads to innovation, as the ample research has shown. With that said, I want to change the conversation regarding

D&I and innovation. For a company to merely survive is to D-I (with a long "i" vowel). It's quite simple what I mean by this. If you look at the fifty companies that were featured in the books *In Search of Excellence, Built to Last,* and *Good to Great,* you will notice that many of those companies are no longer around, including the likes of Circuit City, Kodak, K-Mart and Wang Labs.

All of these companies were highlighted as being great companies, but the greatness at that time didn't mean they would survive. Charles Darwin put it best in his book, *On the Origin of Species.* The strongest or the most intelligent are not the ones who survive. It is the one who is most adaptable and open to change (i.e., the most innovative) who survives. The same is true in companies.

Rob Gonda makes the case for this point in his Forbes article, "Adaptability Is Key to Survival in the Age of Digital Darwinism."[47] He points out that the average age of a company in the S&P 500 has dropped to less than twenty years now from sixty years in 1950s. "It is not the biggest or more financially stable that will survive," he says, "but the ones that manage to adapt to the exponentially accelerating pace of change."[48]

Gonda highlights many of those companies in *In Search of Excellence.* Kodak failed to adapt to the shift from printed photographs to digital photographs. Blockbuster was bested by the likes of Netflix and other digital media companies. The switch from printed books to digital books caught Borders off guard. Sears, a company that so many grew up with and was founded in the late 19th century, quickly fell into last place because it failed to adapt to the multi-channel retail outlet model and the changes in customer preferences. Gonda believes that adaptability quotient (AQ) will become the key predictor of success, besting general intelligence and emotional intelligence. According to the Harvard Business Review, adaptability and the ability to innovate are the new competitive advantage.[49] Thus, increasing adaptability by increasing the diversity of a company's workforce is not only wise, it is critical to survival.

Tony Robbins once said, "Change happens when the pain of staying the same is greater than the pain of change," and this is applicable to the need for adaptability. Although many companies feel that they are open to innovation and change, in fact, the company is not. If you look at the diversity quotient of an organization, companies with a diverse workforce and a high DQ will feel the pain and necessity to change because of their awareness of the world around them—politically, socially, economically, and all of the other rapid changes that are occurring. Those people, and thus that company, are light years ahead of a company or group of people with a low DQ. The low DQ company doesn't even realize that it needs to adapt and change because it is unaware of what is going on in the broader world. It is unaware of the pain that it will inevitably experience by not changing in an ever-changing marketplace.

From a DQ perspective, if you have a group of individuals with a high DQ, they would be able to see things from a variety of perspectives based on their varied experiences and knowledge. When problem-solving or forward-thinking, people with high DQ tend to say: "Well, wait a minute. There isn't just one issue here that we need to address. There are several issues. I see one issue. This group will see another issue, while another will see this a third issue." This varied perspective gives the team a better understanding of what the real problem is and how to address it.

Higher DQ brings a much wider set of experiences, backgrounds, insights, interests, goals, and desires to the team. It also brings a broader history of decisions that went well and those that went wrong. This helps teams build a significantly better approach to what a problem may look like or what an opportunity may look like.

Non-diverse teams tend to have a major issue with blind spots. Going to back to **Image 5.2** we can see that a low-DQ team can't fully calculate the risks because they don't have the experience or background to see where potential issues can occur. It's a narrow-minded focus, and you don't see what is on the periphery—which are the blind spots (area above and below their narrow focal point).

Professor Katherine Phillips correctly recognizes that "generally speaking, people would prefer to spend time with others who agree with them rather than those who disagree."[50] The study also found that the presence of diversity doesn't foster better performance and innovation merely because of the introduction of new ideas; rather, heterogeneous groups outperformed homogenous groups because the presence of diversity yielded "more careful processing of information."[51]

In a homogenous group filled with people who share the same viewpoints and experiences, the mutual agreement is comforting and self-reinforcing. However, all you have is a group of "bobble heads" nodding in concert with each other. In a heterogeneous group, on the other hand, the difference of opinions and disagreements act as catalysts for more meaningful discussion, problem-solving, and issue spotting. Disagreements and discussions can catalyze new ideas. And as Professor Phillips suggests, the new ideas do not generate simply from having a diverse team, but from the *presence of diversity* on the team.

I have seen this happen firsthand when a newcomer is added to the team from a diverse background. Then, the team comes up with two or three new ideas, none of which came from the new team member. Then they say, "Oh, you see? We didn't need to be diverse. We came up with the ideas ourselves." Wrong. The new addition caused a disruption to the status quo and to the alignment of individuals—and, more importantly, to the alignment of thinking. The newcomer changed the dynamic of the group, and the group's thinking had to make room for the new idea or approach. Once again, this phenomenon is difficult to measure exactly, but from my own experience, this is what happens when TRUE DIVERSITY is introduced into a team.

For example, take my team that was charged with launching a new clinical platform for Hepatitis-C against a competitor who'd dominated the market for years. My company had researched African-Americans and Hepatitis-C before the competitor, and we also had data on patients that were co-infected with Hep-C and HIV years before the competitor. Finally, prior to launching the new clinical platform, our team had important information on end-stage liver disease. All of this proved to be a leg up on the competition well before we launched the new platform.

The reason we were ahead of the competition was because of the make-up of our medical team. Chris was a Greek transplant hepatologist who looked at the disease through the lens of a liver specialist. Brian was a clinician who was also an infectious disease doctor. He didn't see the disease as a liver disease, but as an infectious disease to be studied alongside HIV. Luis, who was also an infectious disease physician, is Cuban with a strong interest in minority health. Finally, the other physician, Georges, was Lebanese. When you look at this group, it was a diverse medical team in terms of backgrounds, interests, and specializations. They all approached the problem of the disease from different perspectives. And they certainly did argue about the proper approach.

The arguments on the team went something like this:

One would say, "Hey, it's the liver!"

The other guy would then say, "No, it's definitely the virus. Don't you guys know anything?

That's what I wanted. I wanted debate between the different perspectives so that we could come up with the best possible strategy. Then, an opportunity came to look at programs the competitor was offering to the customers. They offered three different customer assistance programs, each with its own 1-800 number. We saw the opportunity to simplify what they were doing because if we, as well-trained industry professionals, were confused, then the customer was certainly confused, too. Our team came up with one number to satisfy all three functions.

Our single toll-free number solution almost didn't happen. I was told that it was going to be impossible by at least four different people who had deep Pharma marketing experience. They took the idea to expert agencies, and they all said that it was impossible. I don't believe anything is impossible, especially with the right team and people looking at the problem.

I hired a woman with absolutely zero pharmaceutical marketing experience. She was an environmental engineer and looked at the issue through the lens of one. Environmental engineers are taught to analyze an extremely complex contamination situation and try to find the source(s) of the materials. It could be pollutants. It could be particles. Good or bad, the goal of an environmental engineer is to find the sources, and sometimes down to the parts per million in a situation where there are many things going on at the same time.

Everyone thought I was crazy because we had four Pharma "experts" look at the issue and none of them could solve the problem. We were looking at the problem from the wrong angle. We were partnering with pharmaceutical service providers when we should have been looking elsewhere. She advised that we should be partnering with AT&T, and also the people who would be setting up the call and the warm transfer (how to transfer a call from one human to another while maintaining contact at all times with the original caller) for the various services. Warm transfers require a human being to assist in transferring a call from one area to another and cannot be accomplished by simply pressing a number off an automated menu. By working with the right people, she was able to set up a system where patients only had one number to call. On that number, the patient told the operator what they needed, and from there the patient was either called back or warm transferred. She had accomplished what I'd been told was impossible simply because she added a diverse perspective of looking at the problem. It put us light years ahead of the competition.

PUBLIC FACING MESSAGING ABOUT DIVERSITY

While researching this book, I came across two examples of how a company's public and online presence send the right message about the intersection of diversity and innovation. The first really intrigued me because it is for the petroleum industry. At first thought, the image of someone who works in petroleum is pretty singular in the imagination. More male than female. More white than any other race. I polled several people on this question, and the answers were the same. The website PowerPastImpossible.org puts forth a different, more diverse image of the industry. The goal for the visuals on the site is to break the stereotype of what we'd typically think about a petroleum worker.

On the website, the pictures that you see on the home page include women, minorities, and other non-white male workers in the industry. The messaging is that the oil industry has become an IQ industry and the diversity of their industry is leading to innovation. The site shows how you can "see through rock" without making the mistakes of the past practices, and this is a result of having one of the most diverse workforces in the industry. Another innovation that they attribute to diversity is the ability to "subtract" the amount of carbon from different types of oil. By harnessing the brainpower of the expanded industry demographic, they are making significant strides in the way petroleum is mined, collected, and distributed. It's right upfront on the site:

> You may think of roughnecks when you think of the natural gas
> and oil industry, but the industry is becoming more and more
> high-tech every day. The incredible women and men of our

industry – the engineers, analysts, scientists, geologists and more – are using their brainpower to create cutting-edge technologies that make energy development more precise, efficient and safer than ever before.[52]

Another company that fascinated me while I was trying to find companies that utilize diversity to spark innovation was a small company, Ruby Receptionists. The CEO and founder, Jill Nelson, spells out the core values of the company, and when she talks about innovation, it's all about inclusion. According to the site, the Ruby team is a "Founder-led, Diverse Leadership Team."[53] Its commitment to innovation "is fueled by the ideas, dreams, and goals of everyone on our team—customers and coworkers alike."[54] A direct link to the company's core values is prominently displayed on the site, talking about innovation and how that innovation was fueled by inclusiveness.

Now you see why I believe that enough is enough. It's not a matter of whether diversity leads to innovation. It does. The question is whether your company is ready to accept the facts, research, and data to implement a TRUE DIVERSITY strategy that will ensure the company's success and survival. There is no industry that can afford *not* to empower and encourage innovation. Diversity is an essential factor in doing so.

CHAPTER 4:

Dissecting the Pie Graph

"There's something that happens with the collection of a large amount of data when it's… put into a pie chart. You run the risk of completely missing what it's about." —Aaron Koblin

We've all seen pie graphs or charts since the early days of elementary school. Pie charts are generally used to show percentages or proportional data, and usually the percentage represented by each category is provided next to the corresponding slice of pie. Pie charts are good for displaying data for six categories or fewer. In terms of diversity, companies use the pie graph to display the percentage of the various groups reflected in each graph. For gender, the percentage of men versus women, and for race, the percentage of each racial group in proportion to the whole company. Below is a very simple pie chart showing the racial/ethnicity of COVID cases in a particular state.

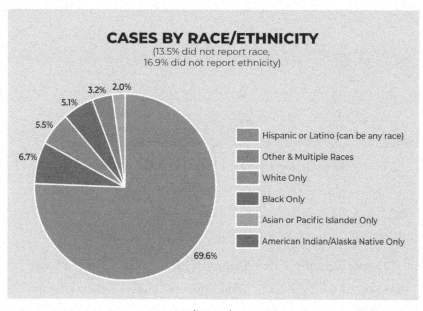

(Image 6)

Pie graphs are helpful tools for a quick snapshot of a company's demographics. However, for the purposes of TRUE DIVERSITY, the pie graph is not an accurate reflection of a company's diversity. You can actually go into each separate slice and further define the group. Below is another pie chart showing gender percentages of a company.

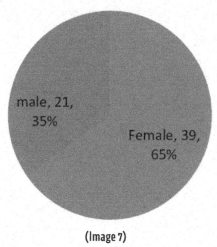

(Image 7)

Let's take a look at the female slice, and you can separate that portion of the graph to create another pie graph. The new pie graph can differentiate amongst the female employees based on their race, country of origin, education, experience or just about anything that you can quantify. In the case below, you see the "percent of women named by race" from the National Women's History Museum.

Named Women by Race

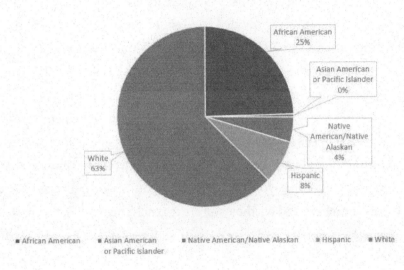

(Image 8)

That is a basic understanding of the pie graph.

As stated, companies typically use pie graphs for diversity purposes during the goal-setting and post-hiring evaluation processes. During the goal-setting process, companies—usually the HR department along with leadership—set a goal to increase a portion of the graph by attracting (and retaining) a diverse workforce. Sometimes, but rarely, there is a little more meat around it with more tangible goals and directives. Regardless of whether the goal, and thus the pie graph, is general or very specific, what it never captures is the actual conversation at the end of the assessment or hiring period, which is a justification I call the "dwindling effect."

Basically, a company sets a goal of increasing the number of women by ten percent at the outset of the hiring process. They want to move the pie graph from thirty percent women to forty, which is an honorable goal. As the process moves forward, the number begins to dwindle because of various hurdles in either attracting female candidates or the perception that there aren't enough qualified female candidates available. Then, the conversations during the dwindling effect start sounding like this: "We have really tight timelines to fill these roles," or "I wasn't provided enough female candidates during the screening process," or "the female candidates that I was given weren't qualified." And in the end, the goal of ten percent has dwindled down to two percent—and has been justified at every step along the way.

As previously discussed, another primary reason why pie graphs don't work is because they represent a two-dimensional approach to a multi-dimensional issue. Pie graphs are birthed from the quota system. It doesn't matter what you think about the utility of quotas or target diversity numbers today; they were extremely helpful in the past to encourage employers to diversify their staffs when they generally did not want to do so.

In 1977, the federal Office of Management and Budget adopted the "Race and Ethnic Standards for Federal Statistics and Administrative Reporting" via Directive No. 15.[55] It set the classifications for race and ethnicity for "record keeping, collection, and presentation of data" in federal programs. It further states, "[t]hese classifications should not be interpreted as being scientific or anthropological in nature [sic]. They have been developed in response to needs expressed by both the executive branch and the Congress to provide for the collection and use of compatible, non-duplicated, exchangeable racial and ethnic data by Federal agencies."[56]

The classifications set forth in Directive No. 15 then became widely used by employers to comply with various laws and regulations, including affirmative action statutes. It led to the use of the corporate pie graph for companies to assess where they stood in terms of race (and gender). It was an easy way to look at whether they were compliant or not. Within ten years of the Directive's passage, however, it became clear to the government that it was merely a start. The Directive did not go far enough in reflecting the TRUE DIVERSITY of the US population, which prompted a revision in 1997.

On October 30, 1997, the federal Office of Management and Budget issued "Revisions to the Standards for the Classification of Federal Data on Race and Ethnicity" (the "Revision").[57] The revision made two major modifications: 1) it separated Asian or Pacific Islanders into "Asian" and "Native Hawaiian or Other Pacific Islander" and 2) changed the term "Hispanic" to "Hispanic or Latino." "The revised standards will have five minimum categories for data on race: American Indian or Alaska Native, Asian, Black or African American, Native Hawaiian or Other Pacific Islander, and White. There will be two categories for data on ethnicity: 'Hispanic or Latino' and 'Not Hispanic or Latino.'"[58]

The revisions recognized that even within a particular race or ethnicity, especially Asians and Latinos, there was a need to further differentiate due to the variations within one race. I believe this supports why the pie graph approach is a lackadaisical strategy for diversity.

Even with the modifications made in the revisions, we all know that it doesn't even scratch the surface of the variations that happen within a racial group itself. For Hispanic or Latino people, we value and acknowledge the differences amongst the cultures that make up the ethnicity. Cubans, Mexicans, Puerto Ricans, and so on all share similarities like the Spanish language, but the cultures are vastly different, even down to how the language itself is spoken.

In China, there are five main dialectical groups with over two hundred dialects. If that sounds like a lot, let's travel to Africa where there are somewhere between 1,500 to 2,000 different languages spoken.

So, putting Latino, Chinese, or African on an application or a pie graph isn't very helpful, especially if the consideration is about the customer and the customer's needs.

Both China and Africa are huge emerging markets for global business, so if you looked at your staffing needs from a pie graph approach, you might miss being able to understand a significant segment of your target customer base solely because of language. A perfect example is when I was in charge of launching a new product for the treatment of Hepatitis B at Novartis. I knew it had a high prevalence in the Chinese-American and Chinese populations. I also knew that within that population there were many language variances. We were able to effectively target and understand the customers because we made sure we hired employees that spoke Cantonese, Mandarin, and other major Chinese dialects. Because our workforce represented our customers in a meaningful way, we were able to gain trust and develop the correct programs. Take a look at the performance of the Hepatitis B product we launched with a TRUE DIVERSITY lens, and then what happened after I was no longer able to lead that brand with a TRUE DIVERSITY approach. The graph shows TRxs (total prescriptions), and it was gifted to me by an employee who missed my leadership.

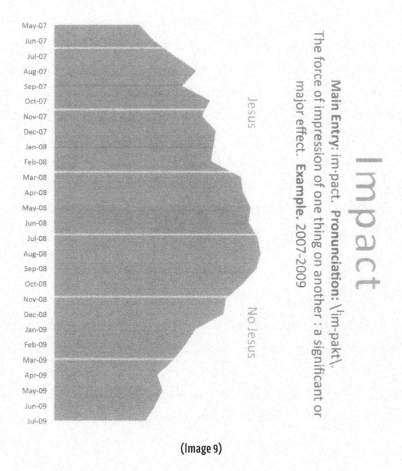

May-07
Jun-07
Jul-07
Aug-07
Sep-07
Oct-07
Nov-07
Dec-07
Jan-08
Feb-08
Mar-08
Apr-08
May-08
Jun-08
Jul-08
Aug-08
Sep-08
Oct-08
Nov-08
Dec-08
Jan-09
Feb-09
Mar-09
Apr-09
May-09
Jun-09
Jul-09

Jesus

No Jesus

Impact

Main Entry: im·pact. **Pronunciation:** \im-pakt\. The force of impression of one thing on another : a significant or major effect. **Example.** 2007-2009

(Image 9)

I understand that the pie graphs are not going away because they're very simple to communicate. But we cannot allow the pie graph to become a company's bible on its annual report that says to shareholders, "We are a diverse company." We must go beyond the pie graph to a multi-dimensional approach to diversity.

As previously stated, the pie graph approach allows a halfhearted attitude toward the whole subject of diversity and inclusion. It supports and reflects short-term mindsets—namely, quarterly and annual performance—that are very restrictive and limited. Thus, your goals are narrow and not geared toward long-term. Say a company sets a goal of hiring X number of Y people by Z date because of an expansion or a product launch. Setting the arbitrary goal is akin to quotas; it is a numbers game. The problem is that setting goals like this doesn't take into account finding employees who fit your marketplace and consumer. The process may take a little longer, but it will have more long-term benefits.

Another reason why the pie graph approach is a distorted view on diversity is because it doesn't delineate where diversity in the company actually is. I know companies where the only highly diverse department is HR. When a minority candidate interviews, he or she sees all of these diverse faces in the hiring process only to realize after taking the job that there is less (or zero) diversity in their functional workgroup.

GOING BEYOND THE PIE GRAPH

One of the fundamental issues with the pie graph approach to diversity is that it's often considered to be an HR issue when, in fact, it should be considered a business issue. Basically, when you set goals based on a pie graph—improving slices of the pie in various categories—it's wrapped into people management. It is an HR appraisal. But if you start looking at how well someone understands the business model, the business strategy, the product and, most importantly, the target consumer, then you're evaluating the employee from a business perspective. It's not just about meeting a quota or improving that slice of the diversity pie short-term. It becomes about having a long-term effect on the business and the consumer.

Making traditional pie-graph identifiers—race and gender—a secondary consideration to your business needs will ultimately yield better results. If you're looking to your customers as your guide in hiring, invariably you will create a diverse workforce. Very few businesses these days have a monolithic customer base. No consumer base is all white and all male. Therefore, instead of looking to hire X number of women or minorities, you should be looking to hire a workforce that reflects the needs and identity of your customer. Trust me, it will yield results that outpace any quota system or target numbers.

My team for Hepatitis C is a perfect example of how hiring processes reflected business needs, which naturally led the team to be diverse in terms of racial and ethnic background. Moreover, the team was diverse in their specialties, education, and experience. Granted, it could have been a bit more gender diverse, but the team was rounded out on the marketing side by a woman who revolutionized the process due to her unique experiences and insight.

If you looked at that same team from a two-dimensional pie graph approach, it might not look as diverse. If we used a pie graph and cut the chart by education discipline prior to joining the team, the chart would simply show a slice of 4 doctors. However, if you went deeper, you would know that each of those doctors had a different specialty, educational background, and point-of-view, all of which added to the team's ability to think about and address the issues surrounding Hepatitis C from a multi-dimensional and holistic perspective. This is what I am emphasizing in the TRUE DIVERSITY approach.

Once your company understands that diversity is a business decision, you must engage a team that understands that the decision is multi-dimensional. This thinking has to start from the very top of the company and be adopted as a paradigm shift for the entire company. It can't only be reflected in a pie graph or chart in the annual statement. TRUE DIVERSITY must be incorporated into the very fiber of the company. From the mission statement to the internal/external corporate communications to the very way the company conducts its business, a multi-dimensional approach to TRUE DIVERSITY must become the company culture.

While researching this book, I came across myriad articles and stories about former retail giants that no longer exist. Atlantic Thrift

Stores, Kmart, Alexander's, Two Guys—they all disappeared. Walmart, however, thrived and continues to grow. (Whatever you may personally think about its retail dominance; it is an undeniable truth).

In a 2011 article for Diversity, Inc., Donald Fan, who was Walmart's Senior Director in the Office of Diversity, highlighted Walmart's commitment to diversity and how that commitment fueled innovation.[59] It is a business-based approach to diversity that doesn't merely look at a pie graph or numbers in a report. Walmart looks at its diversity-and-inclusion matrix to try to understand what's happening in the populations where they decide to open one of their supercenters. They believe that their inclusive culture is an incubator for creative thinking.

Another example is Bank of America ("BoA"). On their website, BoA talks about connecting diversity directly to improving a specific community. They use Baltimore's Tradepoint Atlantic redevelopment as an example where the diversity strategy was business/consumer-based. After all of the socioeconomic issues facing Baltimore and the flight of many businesses from the Baltimore area, Tradepoint Atlantic looked at what their business issues were and they identified the needs of the community. They found that the prevalent need was for Baltimore to be able to compete with ports around the world in a much more cost-effective manner.

To do so, they would need to find a way of bringing multiple companies into a localized center to decrease the transit time to improve on-time processing of the goods being shipped. Bank of America found a 3,100-acre site and financed it to accomplish this goal. They then looked at the surrounding community and determined that there was a diverse workforce of all levels of skill, indicating that the area was a good investment for growth for the company.

The company didn't say, "Hey, we want to expand into Baltimore and we want to make it a really diverse workforce." Instead, the company looked at its business needs and determined that they needed shipping, rail, road, and air links in order to compete in the global economy. It also needed space capable of accommodating various companies and trades in one place. Finally, it needed different types of people with different backgrounds from a wide range of socioeconomic levels to fill those jobs. Based on all of those business needs, BoA settled on Baltimore and the Tradepoint Atlantic site. The initiative brought 17,000 new jobs to the area with diversity across multi-dimensional identifiers, including gender, age, socio-economic status, licensure status, and geographic origin.

THE **TRUE DIVERSITY** *APPROACH*

Companies have used the pie graph because it's straightforward and easy. You can see how many women versus men are in your company pretty quickly. Set a goal to increase that by a certain percentage and then go about the hiring process. For the various reasons already outlined, that is not the ideal approach to diversity. With that said, I acknowledge that the TRUE DIVERSITY approach is not as simple. It takes thought, planning, and in many respects, more time. It isn't a daunting or unachievable task, however. Many companies are applying the TRUE DIVERSITY approach right now even if they don't call it such.

I came across an article on Ideal.com that gives guidance on how to increase diversity during the hiring process. It sets forth six steps that companies can follow to accomplish the goal of a diverse workforce.

According to Indeed, step one is to conduct a diversity-hiring audit on your company's current hiring process. The second step is to pick one metric to improve for your diversity hiring. The third step is to increase your diversity hiring in your candidate sourcing. Fourth, the company should increase your diversity hiring in candidate screening. Number five is to increase the diversity in your candidate shortlist.

Finally, the sixth step is to go back and evaluate your company's diversity hiring metrics.

Sounds great. But in my opinion, it's just a good start. In fact, there's a hugely redundant problem in all of the six steps. How many steps have the word "your" in it? All six of them. It's all internally focused. The only way you're going to change the hiring process and go beyond the pie graph is to change the focus from internal to external. To make sense of this, I like to borrow a saying from a Canadian company called Grizzly Canadian Lager, Lakeport Brewing Company. Their slogan is, "If you're going to be a bear, be a Grizzly." It's time to be a Grizzly bear when it comes to diversity issues. The way to be a Grizzly is to change the company's focus from yours to theirs. From internal to external. From an HR decision to a business decision. From employee to consumer.

You change those questions from an internal to an external focus by first starting with the business plan in mind. Gather the HR department, hiring teams, executives, and management to educate them on who is buying the product. Provide as much cross-department information on who your consumer is as possible. You will need to answer these questions:

1. Who is using the product or service?

2. What do those people like?

3. What is their preferred language(s)?

4. Where do they live?

5. Where do they work?

6. What are the other social and cultural factors generally shared by our customers?

7. What do they do in their spare time?

8. Who best knows these customers?

9. Where do I find the people who best know our customers?

10. Where do the people who know our customers
    best go to school?

Once you understand the answers to these questions, you will better understand the type of applicant pool you need. It is an external and business approach directly tied to your consumer and your users. Therefore, the diversity of your applicant pool should reflect the diversity of your customer. You've gone beyond the pie graph into a TRUE DIVERSITY approach, which will yield better results during the hiring process and beyond.

A TRUE DIVERSITY approach doesn't just look at the initial hiring process, but also promotions within the company for existing employees. I think the issue is that companies tend to focus the diversity strategy on the new employee hiring process and not enough focus is placed on diversity during the promotions process. The step-by-step list provided by Indeed suggests that companies pick one metric to improve for its diversity hiring. Just one metric. It would take forever using this strategy! Once again, it's the death by the gradualism approach that has been failing companies for decades. It is the approach that will leave your company behind in the fast-paced and ever-changing global economy.

I strongly believe that if you're going to make a genuine impact on your company's diversity, then you have to take a hard look at the promotions process. I know I just said the focus should be external, but here is an exception. It's not just about promoting more women and minorities, which should certainly be a goal. It is also about promoting people who understand the business impact of a diverse and inclusive organization. As the studies have demonstrated, this has a halo effect during the new hire process as well. People from diverse backgrounds want to work at companies where they already see diversity. Highly skilled people who know the power and benefits of diversity will also be attracted to your company for the same reason, especially if they see people from diverse backgrounds in positions of power and decision-making.

A pie graph is an easy way to approach diversity. It will not, however, yield the type of long-term results necessary to sustain growth and encourage innovation. The TRUE DIVERSITY approach goes beyond the pie graph by moving diversity from a HR issue to a business issue. It shifts the paradigm of thought from an internal one to an external consideration. Once again, it puts the focus where it should be—on your customer.

CHAPTER 5:

The Hiring Process

"D&I needs to be something that every single employee at the company has a stake in." —Bo Young Lee

By now, hopefully the case for a TRUE DIVERSITY approach is clear. In this chapter, I will provide effective ways for a company to design a diversity strategy that takes into account more than an employee's two-dimensional identity. I will also explore ways companies and human resources departments can implement practices that allow for the application of our TRUE DIVERSITY principles in the hiring process.

THE NECESSITY OF A TOP-DOWN PHILOSOPHY

The single most important factor in building an effective diversity strategy is the commitment of the leadership. Any successful strategy must be derived from a top-down approach, and as such, the company leadership is critical in setting the tone. At the very top levels, a company's executives and leaders need to understand the concept that diversity and inclusion is a strategic business decision, which requires more than a buy-in. It requires real conviction. An executive's "buy-in" says, "Yes, we will implement this strategy." An executive's conviction says, "No, we *need* to implement this strategy."

An executive who has conviction toward a diversity strategy transforms the process from a company merely checking off boxes or simply improving the look of a yearly pie graph. It becomes a part of the company's DNA, and that has to be established at the top levels of company leadership. This type of top-down approach requires leadership to truly understand the business from the employee and customer level. It is a consumer's world, and in order for any company to be successful, you have to tap into the values, beliefs, thought processes, and needs of the community of consumers to which you are selling your goods or services. A deep (as opposed to superficial) understanding of the consumer will drive leadership conviction to diversity and inclusion. Conviction will only come when the person ultimately responsible for the company's bottom line understands that the diverse consumer is actually exponentially more diverse than originally conceived—and whoever understands that concept first will gain market leadership in their industry.

For this reason, before any company embarks on designing a diversity strategy for hiring, the leadership and management should start with a consumer-based business plan. Many companies have moved away from the traditional MS Word document business plan to presentation decks. This is unfortunate because too much is left to the interpretation of slides. The interpretation(s) can become problematic from decision-makers that may not have been at the meeting where the business plan was presented. Therefore, in order to really appreciate the value of a diverse team, I believe that leadership should either write a traditional Word document business plan, or include as many notes as possible in the "Notes" section of the PowerPoint. These notes must include the insights from consumer research and should take into account those diverse populations that make up a large part of the customer base. If the business plan is consumer-focused and takes the company's product or service on a journey through the eyes of the consumer, the target consumer will come to life. The current marketing team should be able to construct the business plan from the consumer's eyes. If they can't do that then, it might be time for a new marketing team.

The purpose of this business plan is to make the target audience actually come to life. To best understand any consumer, you must first understand what problem or need they are trying to solve with your product. You must also know how they acquire and use the product. Once you fully understand the product from a consumer-engagement standpoint, you should build your business plan around it. And one of the best ways of ensuring that your business plan captures the diversity of your customer base is to hire a diverse team.

The reason why this approach works better than the typical or traditional approach to diversity is that your consumers are invariably diverse. It is doubtful that all of your consumers access and use your products in the same way. A TRUE DIVERSITY approach moves away arbitrary quotas or two-dimensional pie chart numbers, because once you know your consumer, you will know what your team needs to be to reflect the diversity of your consumer. Hiring from this approach is business-based and will ultimately lead to greater returns from your employees and for your product.

Here is an example. Let's assume that you want to launch a consumer campaign targeting Hispanics and you want to use a celebrity spokesperson. Who you choose may determine the response to your advertising from different Hispanic groups. For example, if you choose a current or past Hispanic politician (never a good idea, but let's use this for illustrative purposes) as your spokesperson, then you limit yourself to a particular political viewpoint and audience. If you choose a celebrity whose public image is extremely liberal, you have a greater chance of attracting the majority of the Hispanic audience. However, you must keep in mind that you will probably alienate a good portion of the Hispanic consumer base that tend to be more conservative, such as Cuban and Venezuelan consumers. If you don't believe me, try this exercise using two different Hispanic politicians: Congresswoman Alexandria Ocasio-Cortez and Senator Marco Rubio. Both are Hispanic political figures, but are obviously at opposite ends of the political and ideological perspective. Seemingly, the Congresswoman will appeal to liberal Hispanics and the Senator to more conservative Hispanics. You have to know your consumers because just picking a Hispanic for a Hispanic consumer won't get you far if your consumers don't view the spokesperson favorably because of their beliefs. Hispanics, as with any ethnicity or race, are not monolithic and cannot be marketed to as such.

Again, this all begins and ends with the leadership's conviction to create and maintain a truly diverse workforce. Once leadership fully understands the consumer, designing a business-based diversity strategy becomes easier—and even more important. The strategy is now focused on improving consumer outcomes and interaction with your product. Thus, your strategy is specific and pointed versus arbitrary and abstract.

UTILIZE A DIVERSE HIRING TEAM

Even with a top-down approach, a diversity hiring strategy will fail if the management team charged with leading the hiring process (along with HR) is not diverse. If the top-down philosophy is handed over to a non-diverse management team, you lose a great deal of the potential impact. So, the next step in developing an effective diversity hiring strategy is creating a diverse management team that is empowered to drive diversity. A diverse management team will *automatically* introduce changes in the recruitment and interviewing process.

One of the biggest obstacles to diverse hiring has nothing to do with diversity. This obstacle is a functional one: most executives and managers who are in interviewing roles do interviewing and hiring as a part-time job, at best. The hiring process is a small portion of their day-to-day duties, and it often takes a back seat to all of their direct duties in their job description. Unless the company is a startup, hiring executives tend to devote no more than 2-4% of their time to recruitment and hiring. In order to realize the opportunities and advantages from a diverse workforce, we will need to invest more time in the recruitment and hiring phases of our jobs. A better effort must be made for senior leadership to allow managers to free up their schedules to adequately devote meaningful time and effort to the recruitment and hiring process. Once again, this is a business-based decision, and if the company has truly started from the lens of the consumer, justifying the time spent will be easy.

EXPAND THE CANDIDATE POOL

As I have stated many times thus far, a lot of the work that launches an effective diversity hiring strategy starts internally. You must work from a top-down philosophy, develop a customer-focused approach, and engage a diverse management team with the time and resources to devote to recruitment and hiring. All of this internal work will be moot if you continue to look for employees from the same pool of candidates. On paper, many companies' employees look exactly the same. They come from the same group of cities, they went to the same bunch of schools, and their resumes look like carbon copies of each other. Even amongst minorities, there is little to no diversity in background, which means your workforce, even if it looks a little diverse, isn't truly diverse. You must expand the resources the company uses to search for truly diverse candidates.

Here are five simple ways to broaden the search resources for your candidate pool:[60]

1. **Reconsider Job Requirements.** Stop using numbers like "seven years of experience required." Women generally only apply when they feel they meet 100% of the criteria, whereas men apply if they feel they meet 60%.

2. **Nix Bias at the Sourcing Stage.** Are your sourcing strategies yielding a disproportionate of males? White males in particular?

3. **Train to Stop Bias in Screening.** This is where most bias comes in. It can be triggered by names, addresses, etc.

4. **Work to Ensure a More Balanced State.** The University of Colorado's Leeds School of Business found that when four candidates are presented and the ratio is 3:1 (men to women), the woman's chance of being hired is statistically ZERO because they are viewed as a "token"!

5. **Watch What You Do and Say.** Small words can have a major negative impact on the candidate's performance.

EDUCATE THE INTERVIEWERS

I think the next step is to make sure interviewers are educated to ask the type of questions that will yield the TRUE DIVERSITY discussed throughout this book. The actual interview has become a bit precarious with so many companies and interviewers in fear of breaking the law. I actually think that some of the current laws, which were made to protect against discrimination, are in fact working against the concept of TRUE DIVERSITY. For example, you can't ask someone where they were born or where they went to school. (Obviously, this is not allowed because some knucklehead probably used this to discriminate against an applicant.)

I believe there are ways to educate interviewers on how to ask questions that respect the current laws but also lead to hiring a truly diverse workforce. Most of the interview questions I have experienced are closed questions that elicit a closed response. As I said, I understand the perceived safety in this approach in order to stay in step with the laws, but we can train interviewers how to use open-ended questions during an interview process to gain insights into someone's TRUE DIVERSITY and stay within the confines of the law. For example, let's say you have an applicant who received their undergraduate degree abroad and a graduate degree from a US school. Here are a few questions that will tell you more about the diversity of their experience without stepping outside of what is allowed by law:

- Your resume shows that you did some of your schooling outside of the US. Please tell me a little bit about your educational experience in Lebanon?

- I see you earned your master's at NYU. Please tell me a little bit about that experience.

- How does having these two educational experiences help you analyze a business situation?

- What knowledge from your undergraduate experiences in Lebanon did you bring with you to help you complete your graduate studies (in the US)?

Imagine the colorful answers you could receive from questions like these. It's not just about diversity; it's about a better interview with the person.

There are many great resources available to help you educate your interview team and to inspire great interview questions:

1. Diversity Science offers an "Evidence-Based Program" (designed by scientists, practitioners, and professionals) for people at all levels. Diversityscience.org

2. The Gallup Organization offers training that connects culture to competitive advantage. Gallup.com

3. Interview Edge offers training to help identify and deal with diverse interview situations that could be unfamiliar and uncomfortable. Interviewedge.com

4. Jerry Acuff's book, "Stop Acting Like a Seller and Start Thinking Like a Buyer" offers great advice on the use of questions in general. Jerry is a best-selling author and a nationally recognized sales expert. Deltapoint.com

One resource that I found to be extremely helpful was an article published in *Diversity Officer Magazine* entitled "The Top Ten Culturally Competent Interviewing Strategies."[61] Here are the top lines from each of the ten strategies:

1. Allow the applicant to tell you what they can bring to the organization.

2. Determine if the applicant needs any special arrangements (*e.g.* physical access, interpreters, etc.).

3. Prepare questions in advance but have a conversation with the applicant.

4. Be consistent amongst the applicants with your questions. Open-ended questions will provide different responses to explore; however, make sure the exploration is relevant to the position.

5. The best interviewers are good listeners. Make sure you create a space to listen to the applicant and their responses.

6. Make sure your questions are not invasive, irrelevant, or illegal. For example, asking a woman if she intends to have a family is all of the above.

7. Keep a record of your questions and answers.

8. Similar to #6, do not use stereotypes and/or discriminatory language in your questions or your conversation.

9. Make certain that outside recruiters know your requirements and goals.

10. Ensure that a diverse group of employees are part of the hiring decision. (From my perspective, this is the *key* to the hiring work.)

Investing more time crafting effective interview questions will make the overall hiring strategy more effective. Interview questions need to:

- Focus on the challenge/opportunity that is facing the organization.

- Be "open" in nature versus "closed." Closed questions will close down inclusiveness. Open questions cannot be answered by a simple 'yes' or 'no.' Closed questions can be.

- Validate the information in the resume without it being an inquisition. This way the candidate feels trusted and wanted while understanding why the information needs to be reviewed.

SAMPLE **TRUE DIVERSITY** *QUESTIONS*

The following are example questions that can be used during a workshop or a focus group for a marketing project. A quick lesson for fostering inclusive conversations is: "Closed questions close down inclusiveness. Open questions open up inclusiveness." Learn to engage the individual by engaging their mind, heart, and beliefs by setting the proper tone and helping everyone feel valued. Here are some examples of how to achieve this through effectively crafted questions:

- If I gave you and your childhood friends [this task] to accomplish as adults, how might you go about completing it?

- Please explain what would make you choose to do it that way.

- How might your response change with the friends you have met as an adult vs. your childhood friends?

- If you put yourself in the shoes of the design engineer and you wanted to gather market research on a specific design, in your opinion, are these questions the most appropriate questions to ask and why?

- If not, what questions would you ask?

- How would you phrase those questions?

- Why did you phrase those questions in that manner?

- If I wanted to really understand what people from XYZ are thinking about our product/service, how would you suggest we engage them?

- What questions should we ask them?

- What questions should we ask internally?

- In this world of transparencies and instant communications, sensitivities always arise. What sensitive issues do you think we should take into consideration when asking them about our product/service?

- How do you suggest we gather the information we need?

- If we were airing this advertisement or selling this product to your family and friends, how do you think the message or product would resonate with them?

- Why do you think that would be?

- How do you think they would like to see this product advertised and why?

- What aspects of this product do you think means the most to them and why?

- What changes, if any, would you suggest to the messaging, product and/or advertising?

The same approach can be used to legally gain an understanding of a candidate's cultural diversity and innovative thinking during an interview. For example, if the resume shows an undergraduate degree outside of the US and a post-graduate degree in the US, one can ask:

- I see you earned an undergraduate degree in Chemistry at XYZ in Sierra Leone. I am not familiar with the selection process for a school outside of the US, would you mind describing the process that you went through?

- Chemistry is a precise science but there could be many ways to get to the same outcome. In what ways could your varied learning experiences help you approach job challenges of this role?

Again, the most important aspects of developing an effective hiring strategy for diversity is instituting a top-down philosophy were the business case for diversity is made a part of a company's DNA from the very top. Then, creating a diverse hiring team of managers that have sufficient time and resources to devote to the hiring work. Focusing on these two components ensures that the other components of the hiring work will be set up to be effective. Moreover, there are myriad resources available to help your company devise a hiring strategy with a focus on diversity once the top-down, business-based approach is employed and a diverse team of managers are charged with leading the hiring work. And always remember: when interviewing or discussing issues where you want to harness the cultural diversity, use "open" questions where they cannot be answered with a "single word response".

CHAPTER 6:

Building Team Cultural Intelligence

"Cultural intelligence is the capability to function effectively
across national, ethnic, and organizational cultures."
—David Livermore

We have made the case for diversity in the previous chapters, but we must also acknowledge that diversity alone does not drive the bottom line or innovation. Everyone from the C-Suite down to individual team members should develop cultural intelligence in order for a diverse workforce to maximize its potential. In order for diverse teams to function at their peak levels of performance and productivity, leaders and team members with high cultural intelligence indicators are required. A plan is also necessary in the implementation of strategic plans that utilize diversity to prop up profits, productivity, and innovation.

CULTURAL INTELLIGENCE DEFINED

In his book, *Driven by Difference*, David Livermore offers a definition of cultural intelligence that is informative. He says, "Diversity by itself does not ensure innovation. Diversity combined with high cultural intelligence (CQ) does. Cultural intelligence is the capability to function effectively in culturally diverse situations."[62] People with high CQ demonstrate an advanced degree of adaptability across various multicultural situations. Livermore breaks down four components (or, "capabilities") to CQ:

1. CQ Drive: Having the Interest, Confidence, and Drive to Adapt Cross-Culturally.

2. CQ Knowledge: Understanding Intercultural Norms and Differences.

3. CQ Strategy: Making Sense of Culturally Diverse Experiences and Planning Accordingly

4. CQ Action: Changing Verbal and Nonverbal Actions Appropriately When Interacting Cross-Culturally.[63]

According to Livermore, in order to demonstrate high CQ, a person needs to be competent in all four areas. Naturally, everyone has strengths and weaknesses, and the same is true with CQ. However, each can be improved with awareness and attention. Livermore says, "All four CQ capabilities (Drive, Knowledge, Strategy and Action) are a part of culturally intelligent innovation, but the one that is most essential for creating a climate for culturally intelligent innovation is CQ Strategy – the degree to which you consciously address cultural differences to come up with better solutions."[64] This is in line with what has been put forth throughout this book. A TRUE DIVERSITY approach utilizes the diversity of a team to better address the needs and wants of the culturally diverse consumer. Therefore, it isn't enough just to have a diverse team if management and team members don't have high CQ or are unwilling to develop it.

Although cultural intelligence is globally recognized, it is still a modern, evolving term, so there is no universal definition. Thus, it is constructive to review various definitions of the term. The Harvard

Business Review defines cultural intelligence as "an outsider's seemingly natural ability to interpret someone's unfamiliar and ambiguous gestures the way that person's compatriots would."[65] The Cultural Intelligence Center's definition is "Cultural Intelligence, or CQ, is a globally recognized way of assessing and improving effectiveness in culturally diverse situations. It is rooted in rigorous, academic research conducted across more than 100 countries."[66] Finally, the Business Dictionary provides a definition of the term directly relevant to business, stating the CQ is "[a] measure of a person's capacity to function effectively in a multi-cultural environment. Employers and organizations apply CQ as a way to foster tolerance and enhance cross-cultural interactions."[67]

My earlier definition of DQ (Diversity Quotient) is similar to the ones noted above for CQ, but there are some differences. I describe DQ as everything that you're aware of and that has personally impacted you as part of a culture over a given time divided by everything that was happening within that culture over the same time. Therefore, in my definition of DQ, it is clearly defined by time, and the individual must have been personally impacted by the happenings within the culture over that period of time. I have zero disagreements with the topic of CQ (cultural intelligence), and I agree that overall CQ is rooted in a person's adaptability and capability to learn the norms and traditions of another culture. Individuals with high overall CQ have not only been exposed to a wide variety of cultures, but they have also embraced the opportunity to learn and adapt to those norms when interacting with others from different cultures. Cultural intelligence about a specific culture embraces all aspects of that culture, including: 1) dress and customs, 2) communication styles and rules, 3) parenting, 4) religious practices, 5) food and entertainment, and even 6) elder care. In order to fully learn a culture, you must recognize that these norms affect the way individuals from that culture interact with and see the world. Ultimately, it affects how they interact at work and on your team.

The concept of DQ reinforces the effect of *time and the personal impact* on cultural intelligence. In essence, the personal impact can be described as the following: *there is a difference between **understanding** that there is a hunger within a community versus actually **being** hungry while living in that community.* Regarding time, I will reiterate the following example: *the Cuban culture before the revolution is quite different than the post-revolution Cuba.* So, if you only knew Cuba from the 1980s onward, you may have little intelligence of what it was like in the '40s and '50s. In those days, Cuba was a free country, economically stable, a leading exporter of rice, sugar, tobacco, and a favorite vacation destination with modern casinos, theaters, restaurants, etc. Today, Cuba is a third-world nation with a non-recognized currency that is masquerading as a tourist spot.

And, although there are generally respected norms and values across any given culture, no culture is monolithic. Every culture contains subsets that have variant practices. Unless you are completely immersed in a culture, it is a bit unrealistic to expect to fully grasp all of these norms. Instead, you certainly can get a top-line understanding to build your CQ, especially with the people on your team. Two simple examples are the differences seen between Mandarin and Cantonese Chinese or between Northern and Southern Spain.

Cultural Intelligence should not be confused with Emotional Intelligence or "EQ." Your EQ relates to how you deal with all people, and not just people from culturally diverse backgrounds. As such, EQ is a broad umbrella that can be measured whether a team or entity is diverse or not. Like CQ, emotional intelligence has been defined to have four components, but all of the components either have to do with your self-awareness or your interactions with others regardless of the other person's background. EQ is agnostic to the cultural environment. It is solely concentrated on how you understand and react to situations by being self-aware, socially aware, and managing yourself as well as your relationships based on that awareness.

CQ requires a higher level of awareness and interaction. For example, imagine that you are leading a team and your own boss is extremely direct and lacking the level of self-awareness necessary for a high EQ. The team has done a really good job of moving a project along, but the boss finds one tiny aspect to focus on and criticize. Everyone feels defeated because the boss has ignored all of the hard work of the team and decided to focus on the one flaw.

Obviously, the boss has no EQ. As the middle manager, you have to deploy your own EQ to try to diffuse the situation on behalf of the team. You understand that the boss's insensitivity to the amount of effort people have put into the project has caused a negative reaction from the team. The boss lacks the self-awareness and the social awareness to recognize that his management style has impacted the team in this way. Because you have a higher EQ, you step in to make sure the team understands that they are valued and that their efforts have not gone unnoticed. That is emotional intelligence.

Now take the same scenario and look at it through the lens of diversity. Imagine that in the process of the project, the boss has made some insensitive statements, including his lack of concern about childcare issues with regard to working late nights. He has required the team to work on weekends, and at times, that conflicts with the various cultural practices of your team. In this example, scheduling a meeting on a day of religious observation of a key contributor goes beyond a poor EQ. Being aware of these issues is a display of cultural intelligence because CQ goes beyond the broader social awareness of the team and takes into consideration the specific cultures of individual team members. It goes a step further and individualizes the understanding and interactions amongst and between team members while leveraging and not penalizing their diverse backgrounds.

Please do NOT misinterpret what we are trying to do. There are always critical meetings and decisions that must take place in a manner that is agnostic to any variable other than "the business needs." Rather, what I am referring to are those individuals who cannot (or will not) differentiate critical meetings versus routine ones. These are the individuals who always plan travel meetings on Jewish holidays or Martin Luther King Day, and then get upset that some people may not be able to travel or prefer to take those days off. This is an important distinction, and one that must be addressed in any sort of CQ is going to be achieved.

THE IMPORTANCE OF CULTURAL INTELLIGENCE IN THE WORKPLACE

A culturally intelligent management team and workforce are important because of the increasing cultural diversity of consumers and clients. Hiring and developing a team with a high CQ can be a time consuming and costly task, but many studies show that the payoff outweighs the effort. Developing a company with employees who demonstrate high CQ has been said to be worth the effort because it "boosts corporate reputation, achieves better results in cross-cultural organizations, and allows the company to adapt quickly to different environments."[68] In the ever-expanding global economy, businesses need the resources, knowledge, and skill set of high CQ personnel to compete and for international collaboration. The same is true even for businesses that have primarily a domestic customer base as the demographics of the United States are rapidly becoming more diverse.

Cultural Intelligence is also important from a practical standpoint. As a manager, you want your entire team engaged and producing results at the peak of their abilities. The same is true for teammates. By definition, the team works best when it works together. Cultural insensitivity creates unnecessary (and sometimes irreparable) dissension within your team. We want the team to feel as if they are supported by their teammates professionally, and to an extent, personally. Respecting and being open to someone else's culture goes a long way in building the type of trust we discussed in the last chapter.

On any given team, individuals inherently have varied strengths and weaknesses. The goal of the team is to have everyone use the best of their strengths and complement the strengths of their teammates. A well-balanced team has strength in the requisite skill set spread amongst the different team members. That's the core principle of teamwork: no one can be strong in every area, but collectively the team can be.

If I am working on a sales projection and I need to create a financial spreadsheet, I know that doing so is not my strength. Therefore, I have to know that my finance person has my back. Now, if I know that the finance person is a devout Catholic and I need to complete my projections on Good Friday, I better know that I ideally need to get everything wrapped up Thursday (or have an absolute dead stop before noon because 12:00 p.m. to 3:00 p.m. is a sacred time for Catholics on Good Friday).

The importance of cultural intelligence became apparent to me at a very young age. I wasn't even quite ten years old at the time, so I obviously had no idea of the term CQ. As a Cuban growing up in Hudson County, New Jersey, I started to learn that not all Hispanics are the same, and sometimes it seemed that we didn't even speak the same language even though we all spoke Spanish. In Spanish, certain words mean very different things to someone from Cuba, Puerto Rico, Mexico, or the Dominican Republic. For example, what Puerto Ricans call the crusty end piece of a loaf of bread is a term for female genitals in Cuba. I use this example to demonstrate how extreme the cultural differences can be, even within what many perceive to be the same culture of "Hispanic." I can imagine my Cuban father getting completely offended by one of our Puerto Rican friends who was just asking for a piece of bread.

That is a funny version of my first initial understanding of the impact of cultural intelligence. It became even more apparent when my parents moved me out of public school to a Catholic school. In the new Catholic school, there weren't many Hispanics. A lot of my Catholic school friends were Italian, German, and Polish. I remember one day as a little kid; my friend came over to my house to visit. We finished dinner and we asked my dad if we could go to the traveling carnival that was in town.

My dad said, "Sure, as long as you're home by nine o'clock because you have school tomorrow." I thanked my father for granting permission, but my friend complained that we only had two hours. Wow, what a mistake he made! He had no idea that in our culture, you NEVER challenge a parent openly in front of other people, particularly in front of other children. My dad told my friend to go home, grounded me, and said, "I hope you and your friend now understand that two hours is a lot better than zero." My friend didn't realize that what he was saying was considered back talk to my father based on our culture. His behavior would not have been received the same in his home, and being so young, he just didn't have the CQ to know.

Another thing about Cubans of my dad's generation is that they were mostly conservative in their beliefs. They liked order and disliked any form of trouble. As I mentioned, my dad was not a big talker, and he basically had three simple yet direct rules when I was growing up. To recap:

1. Out of school, out of the house.

2. Trouble with the law, out of the house.

3. Get a girl pregnant, out of the house.

Everything we ever faced as kids fit into those three buckets. Culturally, for my father and his generation of Cubans, risk tolerance was low. It was clear what would happen if you broke any of those three rules. You're out of the house.

Later on, I began to notice the impact of cultural intelligence on success. By the time I went to high school, I was back in the culturally diverse public school. My observation was that those groups of kids who were in diverse environments in terms of their school friends and in their classes generally did better than students who were not. The extremely high IQ kids who were in only honors or advanced classes got great grades, but to some extent, they lacked EQ or CQ because they tended to be loners or surrounded only by other high IQ kids. I've actually run into some of them over the years and they haven't fared as well as other kids who might not have had straight "A's" but had really diverse experiences.

Our high school group was diverse in every way you could think of. Although there were many Cubans, there was a blend of Blacks, other Hispanics, Whites, and Asians. We even had some Asian Cubans. Our group also had a mixture of IQs, different EQs, varied success in terms of grades in school, and different cultural and ethnic backgrounds. Looking at the success of our group as a whole, we all did quite well. Some have built successful electrical or plumbing businesses still in Hudson County with five or more trucks, some have owned and operated successful businesses such as liquor stores, clothing boutiques, shoe stores, real estate, travel and insurance agencies, and so on. There were a significant number of us who went off to medical, pharmacy, and other professional schools. Of course, it was not a one hundred percent success rate, as some members of our group encountered challenges along the way that derailed them. Overall, however, our very diverse group with an inherently high cultural intelligence turned out to be very successful. Interestingly enough, those who did not do well is because they failed to develop their cultural intelligence as it related to the world around them. They chose not to understand that cultural intelligence is a two-way street (actually, more like a Los Angeles intersection with many different avenues/highways of information).

My point is this: as minorities, we have our obligation to acquire the education and skills needed to properly integrate into society and use our diversity to flourish. This beautiful country has given us boundless opportunities—no one owes us anything, and we owe it to ourselves to be successful and independent. We need to leverage our innate CQ, add skills or formal education to it, and become the best that we can be. That is what we owe to the next generation.

BUILDING OR IMPROVING CQ

The good news is that given time and effort, you can build or improve your cultural intelligence. It doesn't matter who you are or where you are from; the first step in building or improving CQ is a desire to do so. When it comes to business, it is clear that possessing a high CQ is an invaluable asset in relating to your team, the consumer, and the global economy. The higher CQ you have, the more effective you will be in business.

After you've made the commitment to build or improve your CQ, the next step is assessing where you are presently. We all have various CQ levels depending on our culture or situation, but you must assess your overall CQ level to determine your ability to work and related amongst various cultures. David Livermore's four components of CQ (Drive, Knowledge, Strategy and Action) are an effective way to assess your current CQ. Like EQ, everyone will have areas of CQ strength and areas for growth. Be honest with yourself about where your strengths are and where you have the opportunity to improve.

After your self-assessment of your current CQ, you can then engage some tools that are available to expand the assessment. A quick online search will provide a wide range of tools from academic self-assessment tests to those used by HR professionals. Companies like

Coca-Cola are now specifically looking for leaders and managers with high CQ. Coca-Cola even tests the CQ of every participant in its "high potential leader program" through the Cultural Intelligence Centre (another great resource to test your own CQ).

In 2012, the Chartered Institute of Personnel and Development (CIPD) and the Society of Human Resource Management (SHRM) conducted a study to determine the best ways to build and improve CQ for employees within companies and organizations.[69] The study found that the best way is to tailor the program to a company and team's specific needs and knowledge gaps. The study confirms that there is no one-size-fits-all approach to building or improving CQ.

In my experience, I have found the best way to build and improve CQ is to immerse yourself in a culture by either living in the community or some form of intentional, ongoing, and direct contact with the culture you're trying to learn. The more you immerse yourself in other cultures, the higher your specific CQ and overall CQ will be. If the goal is to expand and grow your business in the Midwest, the best thing to do is to go to the Midwest. If you can't immerse yourself in the actual region, then you should surround yourself with people who have intimate knowledge of the region. Let me give you a funny and interesting example. If you've ever been to Little Havana in Miami and went those little cafes with the side-service windows, then you may have witnessed the cultural difference in something as simple as coffee. Order one of those Cuban coffees and give it to a non-Cuban person who has never tried Cuban coffee. Then watch their reaction. Every time that I introduce someone to Cuban coffee, it's always the same reaction—their faces light up and the pleasure from the taste of the coffee consumes them.

Then, the non-Cuban goes home and tries to make it for himself or herself in their espresso machine. Needless to say, they fail miserably because it has nothing to do with the espresso machine. If you understand the culture, then you know it is all about the little tin cup the barista uses. A Cuban barista uses that tiny tin cup to make Cuban coffee by putting in four to five teaspoons of sugar in the cup. When the machine starts to make espresso, the barista puts the cup underneath. As soon as the first few drops of coffee drop into the cup, he or she takes the tin cup out, puts another little tin cup underneath to capture the rest of the coffee. The barista then takes a spoon and beats the sugar and initial coffee drip into a thick, light brown foam. Finally, the barista takes the coffee from the second cup, pours it into the cup that has the foam, and from there, the barista pours that into a tiny espresso cup for you to drink. Well, the first thing your brain senses when sipping a Cuban coffee made this way is the foam. The foam is high in sugar, and the sweet taste buds are on the tip of your tongue—a perfect pairing! The art of making a Cuban coffee is as essential to our culture as anything else.

Although I believe that travel to and immersion in a culture is by far the best way to improve your CQ, you can also do so closer to home. Most major cities have neighborhoods where diverse cultures are concentrated. From Chinatown to Koreatown to Little Italy to Little Havana, metropolitan cities can offer you the same culturally immersive experience that international travel can.

Within your workplace, there are also opportunities to immerse yourself in a culture with your co-workers. A direct and hands-on experience with your co-workers will serve to improve your CQ with a one-on-one approach. Ask your co-workers to engage over lunch or coffee by explaining that you're seeking to improve your knowledge of their culture. Most people welcome the opportunity to educate people about their culture if approached in a respectful way. The key is to develop a plan that is personal to you and your professional goals.

From a leadership/management perspective, I find that improving team CQ begins with hiring. It all starts with hiring diverse people from diverse backgrounds—in other words, going beyond the two-dimensional pie graph. Then, a leader must create the environment where those diverse team members feel empowered to contribute. Too often, I have found that managers believe that adding the diverse members to the team is all that needs to be done. And almost always, the burden of building and improving cultural intelligence for the team lands on the newest, more diverse teammates.

It is the manager's job to spend time educating and encouraging the team to build their CQ with the help of the new team members, but not as their responsibility or burden. The existing members of the team must also understand that when you bring one or two diverse people, they may not initially feel forthright in expressing their opinions or sharing their backgrounds. It is common for any new member of a team to be hesitant at first until they discover the team's dynamics. This is especially true for minorities and women who are new to a team that doesn't have a lot of diversity.

One of the most effective ways that I have integrated new members from diverse backgrounds into my teams is by creating a team conversation utilizing open-ended questions in group settings. Open-ended questions allow for the responder to provide an answer based on their interpretation and experience. For example, "That's a good thing, right?" will likely yield a closed answer, especially if asked by the boss. On the other hand, the question, "What do you think about that approach?" opens up the conversation. Furthermore, not assuming that one person on your team can speak for their entire race, gender, or ethnicity is key to making sure you don't alienate diverse team members.

I cannot stress enough the importance of learning how to ask questions. Here is an example of a horrible question (although I have heard it exactly as I type it here): "What do African-Americans think about this?" Ouch, it still hurts me thinking of when I heard it. The person who asked the question said to me that he thought he was being "inclusive" by asking for their opinion. Here is a better way of fostering inclusiveness: "Based on your experiences, how do you feel that this will be received by African-Americans, and why?" This question capitalizes on their diverse experiences and honestly tries to solicit their insights. You are not only creating the right environment for diverse opinions and feedback; you are also training the other team members to do the same.

You must also educate your team on the difference between cultural sensitivity and cultural intelligence. In my opinion, cultural sensitivity by itself is just another PC enforcement code term. It forces people to walk on eggshells, and then when the eggshells crack, you force an entire organization into a (usually ineffective) mandatory compliance program. As long as we're focusing solely on cultural sensitivity, the cycle won't end. Cultural sensitivity and cultural intelligence are NOT the same. Cultural intelligence allows you to learn how to communicate with people without the fear of insulting, alienating, or threatening other people. Through education and development of your CQ, you will move from sensitivity to actual understanding and empathy.

Here are a few questions that I believe can catalyze a conversation on your team with new (or not so new) members from diverse backgrounds in an effort to build team CQ.

Question #1: We have a problem to solve. We will try solving this as kids because children are often more creative problem solvers than adults. Can you approach this problem from the creative mind of a child? The question gives the responder permission to talk about their upbringing, but it also inherently allows for them to introduce their cultural diversity to the group without putting them on the spot. You also learn more about the individual and their childhood environment, thereby creating more room for genuine connection. Invariably, you have allowed new ideas to enter the conversation based on the diversity of your team members.

Question #2: "If I made you the design engineer for this product, what changes would you consider making? Can you explain why you would make those changes?" By personalizing the open-ended question, you will discover more about the person than a closed question. It also will inform you and your team about how the new team member processes issues and what they bring to problem-solving from their background.

Question #3: "Please look at the messaging that we are trying to communicate to our customers. If you were communicating this message or selling this product to your parents, what changes, if any, would you make to the message and why?" Now, you're asking the team member to provide feedback not only from his or her own culturally diverse lens, but also from how they understood their parents to interact in the world (and how they would interact with your product). It's a homerun, especially if your diversity hiring was with your consumer in mind. You don't need a focus group to conduct market research for thirty minutes with the team member's parents (i.e., your target consumer); instead, you have someone who has known them for twenty plus years. The learning capital you derived from these questions will be invaluable to your team and the business as a whole. It has also intrinsically built the team's CQ. You enrich and change your organization with the types of questions used to garner the most informed responses from your employees.

ENCOURAGING CULTURAL AUTHENTICITY IN THE WORKPLACE

Cultural authenticity, as a term, is a bit of a misnomer when applied to people. Generally, the term was adapted to evaluate whether a piece of literature, film, or art was authentic to the culture it proposed to represent or illuminate. In the context of business, the term has been used to identify whether employees, typically from culturally diverse backgrounds, show up in the workplace authentically to their culture (or are even allowed the space to do so). My definition of being culturally authentic is how you live your life in relation to the cultural norms of your background. With that said, we all evolve such that our experiences shape how we show up at work and home. What you don't want is for diverse members of your team to put on a "mask" at work that is inauthentic to who they really are or their culture. Cubans outside of Cuba have a word for this: "arrepentido." The most obvious ways this shows up is a Cuban who is offended when people speak to him in Spanish even though the setting may be appropriate, or a Juan that only allows you to call him John and is offended when you don't. (If you think Juan is hard, try growing up with my name, Jesus.) In fact, you want to encourage employees to be culturally authentic to drive innovation through diverse insight and information.

You have to also understand that many minorities and women fear being culturally authentic because they have been told they must fit into a "corporate culture." Quite frankly, corporate culture means you're endorsing an exclusive culture because what you're saying by definition is, "If you don't fit within this culture, you don't fit." A uniform corporate culture by definition is exclusive. Instead, we should be talking about corporate norms that will guide and dictate the proper protocol and behavior.

We must understand that many minorities have been forced to "code switch" (changing language and actions to emulate the majority) their entire lives, and creating an environment where they are free to be culturally authentic may prove difficult. The point is not about merely about the outward expressions of culture—i.e., dress or speech—it is about empowering employees to have and express cultural pride, courage, and authenticity in leadership and in decision-making. It is creating a space where your team feels confident in expressing a culturally-based opinion about your product, service, or business decision. Without and employee having the empowerment to be culturally authentic, you lose many of the benefits of having a truly diverse workforce in the first place.

Helping managers create this environment doesn't have to be difficult, so long as we teach managers to "identify and reward." Rewarding is much more complicated than it actually sounds. In fact, sometimes we actually reward negative behavior without recognizing what we are doing, so let me introduce two "Reward Rules" that I teach every manager who works for me. These two simple rules apply to 99% of all management issues that you may encounter.

Rule #1: Never reward bad behavior. If someone is being exclusive or makes a negative remark, don't reward the bad behavior by allowing them to get off the hook. You address the bad behavior and how it impacts the team as well as the individual from a cultural impact perspective. Now, how you address the situation will determine if the recipient internalizes the desired change or if the recipient becomes more resistant. For that reason, some coaching can and should be done in public, but the second it starts to move to a counseling discussion, it is probably best done in private. Conversely, please note that "rewarding good behavior" in public often leads to others following the behavior that was just rewarded.

Rule #2: Never punish good behavior. Suppose an employee submits a great report on a religious holiday but cannot be in the office to explain the report. Additionally, the employee makes herself available via the phone, but only for a few hours. The employee's family is upset to some extent because she has not been observing the Holy Day. If the manager is upset about the employee not being at work, he or she is displaying poor CQ by not recognizing:

119

- The quality of the report

- The fact that it is a Holy Day

- The impact that the work is having on the family that day

The manager in this example will contribute to that minority employee being a "flight risk," which means that the employee may leave the team or the company entirely if the issue is not resolved. Remember that during many exit interviews, minority employees do not say specifically "what the manager did"; rather, they describe "how the manager made them feel." I propose that in many, if not most, of these situations, a lack of CQ is at play.

A good manager never punishes good behavior. This is such an important point that I would like to share a non-diverse situation to further demonstrate the point.

Scenario

- You invite your fourteen managers to
  a meeting that starts at 8 a.m.

- You provide breakfast in the room from 7 a.m. – 8 a.m.

- The clock strikes the 8 a.m. start time and
  two managers are not there yet

Q1: Do you wait for them to arrive or do you start the meeting? If you wait, you have just punished the ones who made it on time (punishing good behavior) and you have let everyone know that your expectations are that you can come in at whatever time you make it.

- They come in together ten minutes late

Q2: Do you allow those coming in late to grab breakfast prior to sitting down and joining the meeting? My answer, you cannot. If you allow that to happen, you have punished those that were there with enough time before the start of the meeting to grab breakfast. You have also rewarded those who were late by allowing them to take their time to get something to eat. Sorry, they can wait for a break to get something to eat or drink. If you choose not to take my advice, don't be surprised if at future meetings more people come in late and help themselves to breakfast at the cost of the ones that were there on time!

More proactive ways to encourage cultural authenticity require a bit more work. For instance:

- Organizing multi-cultural days for the entire office

- Coordinating cultural lunches and dinners

- Hosting your holiday party at diverse restaurants

These activities are not super easy to pull-off, but they are also not extremely difficult, so I view these as mid-level efforts that help create cultural awareness and encourage cultural authenticity, all in an effort to raise your team's CQ.

The hard stuff is utilizing both formal and informal communication channels to raise awareness, recognition of the project, and how it was accomplished in this environment of cultural inclusiveness. As a manager, you could communicate the positive impact to your immediate team or more broadly across the organization. You can do that by generating internal case studies of how inclusiveness led to a better solution for your team and, ultimately, led to a better product.

You can also look to invite employees outside of your team to participate in projects where their diverse backgrounds will improve the outcome. Beyond your core group of people, you reach out to the organization to see who would volunteer to bring their diversity to your team to garner more ideas and increase innovation. This not only helps your team, but it also gives the other employee a platform to showcase their willingness to support the company's goals beyond their direct job description

Overall, CQ is paramount to the successful integration, inclusion, and utilization of a diverse team. Individual members of your team need to be encouraged to build and develop their CQ in a genuine way and, as a manager, you need to implement strategies to encourage the expression of culturally diverse ideas into the work and the workplace.

CHAPTER 7:

Identifying & Overcoming Bias

**"It's not at all hard to understand a person; it's only hard to
listen without bias." —Criss Jami**

You have biases. I have biases. We all have biases. Our brains are
wired to have biases for very primal reasons of selection. Understanding
that on a basic level allows us to operate from a place of solution
rather than a place of blame and shame. We will discuss bias in more
detail later in the chapter, however, let's start with some fundamental
definitions and truths about bias. A bias is an inflexible, positive or
negative, conscious or unconscious belief about a particular category
of people.[70] Discrimination, especially in its disguised form of hidden
biases, is responsible for hiring discrepancies, uneven pay, and unfair
access to career training that would promote or advance employees.
Learning to identify hidden bias is the first step toward eliminating bias
from the workplace.

As stated above, bias is a natural state of the mind found in *every*
human being. Bias was primary to our basic ability to differentiate
between friend and foe. Believe it or not, the brain has three to four times
as much space dedicated to identifying threats than opportunities.[71]
We have over 150 different types of known biases, and all of them are

rooted in the anatomy of our brains.[72] "Biases are part of what keeps us sane and able to process the enormous amount of information that we are bombarded with at any point in time."[73] There is so much activity occurring in our brains at any given point (11 million bits of information, of which we can only process 40), and our brains need the ability to process data quickly. In order to do so, much of the processing is done unconsciously. Here are three ways that our brain processes data unconsciously: 1) delete (erase and disregard information); 2) distort (change information to suit our needs); and/or 3) generalize (associate information with stored information) in order to handle all of those millions of bits of information we are processing at once.[74]

For these reasons, the most common form of bias in the workplace is implicit or unconscious bias. "You can think of unconscious bias as the cognitive equivalent of muscle memory, coming into play when we are faced with gaps in our own personal experience."[75] Unconscious bias is unintentional, and when we approach workplace bias assuming that most bias is unconscious (aside from blatant prejudice and discrimination), we can be proactive instead of reactive. This proactive approach helps us prevent anger or hurt feelings, and since we are all inherently biased, there is an even greater case to approach the issue from a positive stance. The underlying business case for identifying and addressing bias is to preclude segments of the workforce from being unfairly "excluded from experiences and opportunities for which they are qualified."[76]

IDENTIFYING BIAS IN THE WORKPLACE

First, you and your team must accept the fact everyone has biases. This acceptance takes the pressure off of any individual person because the entire team shares it. Anyone on your team who is interested in finding out more about their hidden personal biases can take one of Harvard University's Project Implicit Bias Tests. You'd be surprised to know how many people don't realize that we all have biases. These tests help us to see where our own specific biases lay, and they provide the opportunity for personal growth.

As an executive or manager, an organizational approach to identifying bias in your workplace is a better approach than individual departments conducting their own programs. The best place to start is always at home. You must first identify your own biases. Harvard researchers found that "70% (possibly even higher) of hidden biases are directed towards African-American, the elderly, the disabled, and overweight individuals."[77] Minorities exhibit the same propensity for bias against these (and other) specific groups that tend to experience the most bias. Our society has consistently painted a negative picture of these groups of people, which has shaped our conscious perceptions as well as our unconscious biases. However, depending on who you are and your background, the majority of your biases may exist elsewhere. Without first doing an honest assessment of your own bias structure, you will not be able to advance your team or company.

As a scientist, one thing I love about data is that the numbers don't lie. Whether you're in HR or just a manager trying to improve the diversity, equality, and inclusion of your team, you should take a look at the hiring data available to you. A natural starting point is to look at your core team solely by the numbers. Assess the diversity of your team first and then look at the numbers of the overall organization. An assessment of the data will reveal if and where there are areas of opportunity to improve the diversity of your workforce. It will also provide very accurate indicators of where your organizational biases are. According to the CareerCast Diversity Network, "Hidden biases will immediately pop up as gaping holes, glaringly obvious gaffs in pay discrepancies, and well-deserved promotions that have slipped by the noses of those in charge."[78]

Next, take a look at company literature to see if it is written with unconscious bias embedded into the language. Everything from job descriptions to manuals to company-wide announcements should be evaluated for bias. Now that we understand that bias is universal and typically unconscious, reviewing written correspondence from this awareness allows you and your organization to correct those instances where those unconscious biases have crept into the company's written work products.

Obviously, there are many ways to identify bias from an organizational level because bias occurs in so many different ways. The above are merely examples of areas to examine. The key is to be aware of your bias with the understanding that the first step in overcoming bias is awareness.

Let me share a personal story of how awareness shaped my consciousness around bias. As you know, I am a conservative Cuban dad who had some pretty strong worldviews based upon the way I was raised and the environment in which I grew up in Hudson County, New Jersey. Despite my exposure to various cultures in my childhood neighborhood, it was not enough to prepare me for the on-the-job training I received parenting three outgoing, opinionated, and outstanding girls. I credit them for giving me a PhD-level education on raising kids, understanding when my cultural biases were getting in the way of raising them in New Jersey, and how to be more inclusive in general.

As a dad, I had to be inclusive raising my girls because it wasn't just work; raising my girls was my main job on this planet. For me, I had to start asking myself the question, "Am I thinking like a dad?" Or more specifically, "Am I thinking like a Cuban dad?" The question helped me remember that: A) they are girls, B) they are being raised in an American culture and things are different, and C) they also have a mom that cares for them dearly and who may have a different view. I had to know when my bias went up and when my filter was distorted.

A funny example (or at least I think it's funny—my girls might think differently!) was the year the NY Jets had just lost to the Oakland Raiders in a playoff game. (I am a die-hard Jets fan, so this is where you're supposed to feel bad for me.) A young man had called for my oldest daughter as the game was ending and asked, "Is Desiree home?" I said, "Yes." I waited. I heard silence, so I hung up the phone. The young man calls back, "Is Desiree home?" I said, "I thought I answered that question already?" For a second, I felt really bad, then the kid got the courage to ask a follow-up question. "Can I talk to her please?" I wouldn't completely let it go and replied, "Now, that's a different question." My daughter heard that part of the conversation, and needless to say, she wasn't too happy with me. As I entered my post-Jets-loss pity party in my study, I realized that I had acted like an idiot because I allowed the following filters to bias my thoughts:

- Cuban dad filter: That's my daughter, stay away

- Jets fan filter: It's OK to act like a brat after being eliminated from the playoffs

I share that story when talking about bias to other people because there is no better way to understand biases than to admit your own biases. Doing so helps create a safe space for other people to admit their own. Awareness is the first and most necessary step to overcoming bias.

OVERCOMING BIAS

It might seem contrary to many of the ideas and premises presented in this book, but one thing is clear: diversity training over the years has not worked, or at least not to the extent they thought it would. A Harvard University study that surveyed over 800 companies across thirty-one years concluded that diversity training had "no positive effects in the average workplace."[79] We might as well throw in the towel and accept that none of this will work, right? Not so fast. What we know now is that traditional diversity training does not work for many reasons.

Researchers Frank Dobbin, Alexandra Kalev and Anderin Kelly believe that, "When it comes to influencing how people act toward one another in the workplace, behavioral science gives us a general rule of thumb: Information doesn't change behavior."[80]

Human beings are more influenced by our environment than we are from being fed information. Most of us often learn by doing or from watching other people than we do from consuming information. Charlotte Blank, chief behavioral officer of Maritz, says, "[W]e humans are much more influenced by our environment, including the programs and policies we use to guide and implement our workplace decisions. [sic] Don't bother appealing to reason or attempting to change implicit bias. Focus on de-biasing the system, instead."[81]

Blank puts forth five behavioral solutions that can be utilized, two of which are worth discussing in the context of hiring:[82]

1. **Blind Yourself**. Once again, the best place to start is with the man or woman in the mirror. If we accept the fact that we all have implicit and unconscious biases that are difficult to overcome because they are embedded in our minds, we can take steps to mitigate our own biases during hiring. The hit television show, "The Voice" is a great example of how blinding our biases creates more opportunities for people who would have been prejudiced because of them. On the show, the judges have their backs turned away from the stage and they solely cast their initial vote for a contestant based upon the person's voice. The result is a far more diverse contestant pool of various ethnicities, races, shapes, sizes, and hues. The same can be accomplished during hiring. You can

(and should) employ measures that remove names and other indicators from resumes before you review them. Thankfully, there are software tools that will do the heavy lifting for you.

2. **Give your gut a break**. You know the saying, "Always trust your gut," and I say that is true in most things. However, your gut opinion about a particular candidate can be (and usually is) rooted in your unconscious biases. Trusting your gut about someone takes into account all of the external factors about the candidate that have been informed by stereotypes, other people, or any factors that has underscored your implicit or unconscious bias. Making decisions based on the data or a performance test replaces the traditional "trust your gut" or "who do I want to have a beer with" approach to hiring.

As with everything we have discussed in this book, the work of TRUE DIVERSITY goes beyond hiring. Being aware of and overcoming bias is paramount to having an equitable and inclusive workforce. "Diversity is getting asked to the party, while inclusion is getting asked to dance at the party," says Dr. Heidi Grant-Halvorson of the NeuroLeadership Institute. And she is correct.

From the outset, leadership has to make it clear that identifying and overcoming all of our unconscious biases is a priority for the company. They can start by making a company-wide announcement (if this hasn't been done already) acknowledging the fact that every employee has bias and stating that the goal is to mitigate these biases and their effect on the workplace. Then, leadership can make an organization-wide assessment of individual bias via elective testing and/ or anonymous surveys sets the motion forward. They can make it clear that the feedback will be used to help the company develop programs and an approach to the issue that is based on the needs and views of the employees. It sends a message of inclusion across the board, which is the underlying goal of this effort.

In reality, most people are absolutely surprised at how unaware they are of their implicit and unconscious biases. In fact, when such biases are pointed out, many people are generally surprised that their actions and responses demonstrate unconscious bias (even though this is hard for women and minorities to believe). This holds true for minorities as well as non-minorities.

For instance, a group of researchers analyzed a popular French grocery chain for mangers' implicit and unconscious bias toward minority and women cashiers. (I may have worked for one of those French bosses...just kidding!) Utilizing the Implicit Association Test, the researchers found that the cashiers underperformed when they were working under managers who exhibited high indicators of unconscious bias. The same group of employees was almost 10% more efficient in their performance when they were working under managers with lower unconscious bias indicators. As Sabel states, "Women and minorities are consistently given lower performance ratings for the same quality of work. They are underrepresented in management roles [and] older workers are assumed to be technically challenged."[83] All as a result of unconscious bias of which, by definition, the managers were unaware.

Experiential and environmental training is the best way to build bias awareness.[84] As previously stated, traditional diversity training has been proven to be ineffective. Individuals must feel that it is their choice to participate in training, and the best training is always an organic and real experience in a diverse environment that builds empathy. There are also empathy exercises that build empathy by asking participants to "walk a mile in another person's shoes," so to speak. These exercises are also called "perspective-taking" activities. Whichever method you use to build awareness, it has to be organic and crafted to your team or audience.

To that end, the more opportunities you create for co-workers to interact with each other in settings and situations where they are allowed to be social and express their culture, the more you will create chances to overcome bias. Often, unconscious bias is rooted in a lack of knowledge of another race, ethnicity, gender, or sexual orientation. Humanizing the individual separate and apart from the group stereotypes in which the biases are rooted provides one of the best ways to overcome bias. When you get to know a person one-on-one, it is often very hard to see that person through the lens of your bias and/or stereotypes.

Role models and mentors also provide an organic way to overcome unconscious bias. Organizations that have effective mentorship programs that connect people from diverse backgrounds inherently begin to breakdown bias barriers. This is particularly the case when the mentor is a person from a diverse background. To that same end, highlighting the achievements of individuals from diverse backgrounds throughout the organization also tends to create a 'halo effect,' which has been shown to diminish the impact of unconscious bias. When people see others from diverse backgrounds that don't fulfill the stereotypes and assumptions that fuel their unconscious biases, it undermines the basis for the bias.

Finally, Charlotte Blank has an idea that I like. She says, "lead like a scientist." The data does not lie. If you are implementing a program or policy design in a way that it can be objectively tested, then you should test it to determine whether or not it achieved the intended goal or effect. Research institutions like MIT are implementing data-based approaches to improving diversity, equality, and inclusion by reducing bias and measuring the results. Within twelve years, the university doubled the number of full-time female faculty in STEM research by designing a program to review gender bias and then analyzing the data along the way to improve the effect of gender bias in their faculty stats.

I conducted my own informal study that was far less scientific, but definitely real-life and experiential. It once again involved my three girls and their friends. An event literally over "spilled milk" caused me to look at my behavior and identify what biased filter was I using at the time. (Probably a filter of perfection and a compounding filter of toughness). One night at the dinner table, my middle daughter accidentally spilled a glass of milk. As I watched the milk drip from the table to the floor I reacted like a caveman. I yelled at her; pointing out the obvious that the milk had been spilled. When I looked over at her, she was motionless and scared until she began to cry. My heart stopped because I realized that I had hurt my daughter's feelings. It made me cry even louder than she was crying because I felt so badly for reacting the way I did literally over spilled milk. Although unpleasant at the time, I am a better person for going through the experience. I hurt one of my daughter's feelings over what—spilled milk? Thank you, Lauren, for making me a better person.

As I learned to be more aware of my own unconscious biases, it helped me relate better to my daughters and their friends. I take great pride in the fact that I became one of the go-to parents for some of my kids' friends. Don't get me wrong; their friends still viewed me as a "tough parent." (Just ask my oldest daughter's husband who met me while they were in high school.) But over time, I became a person who could recognize when I was applying my biases. This allowed me to be more empathetic to where my girls were coming from, and thus, I was more empathetic to them and their friends.

Isn't this what we need to do in our professional lives? I say, yes, it is. We must identify and overcome our biases in the workplace so that collectively we can meet the needs of our customers.

CHAPTER 8:

The Beauty of Ideation
With a Diverse Team

"A lot of different flowers make a bouquet." —Proverb

You get better ideas when those ideas don't come from a homogenous group. Varied experiences, information, education, and upbringing make the ideation process more dynamic. A dynamic ideation process leads to dynamic innovation. The research and history back up these bold statements. For instance, Swedish-American entrepreneur Frans Johansson wrote a book in 2004 entitled, *The Medici Effect: Breakthrough Insights at the Intersection of Ideas, Concepts and Cultures.*[85] Johansson coined the term "The Medici Effect," which is now used throughout various industries to describe innovation that happens when disciplines and ideas intersect. Five hundred years ago, the Medici dynasty rose in prominence and power during the Italian Renaissance. The family made its fortune in the early banking industry and used its fortune to support artists, thinkers, and philosophers, and the family is widely credited for launching the Renaissance era.

The Medicis didn't intend to start the Renaissance, however. The family's practice of inviting painters, sculptors, poets, philanthropists, scientists, philosophers, financiers, and architects into their homes to work or simply socialize over dinner contributed to the expression of diverse ideas. At any given point, names such as DaVinci, Michelangelo, Donatello, Botticelli, and Galileo Galilei were gathered together with artists, scientists, bankers, philosophers, lawyers and politicians to discuss the issues of the times and the future. Innovation was bred from the diverse thoughts from a wide range of disciplines and backgrounds. The family brought the best minds and the best people they could find, igniting a revolution that inspired unprecedented innovation, invention, artistry, and creativity. This was the Medici Effect.

In *The Medici Effect*, Johansson further explores how "disruptive innovation" can come from people outside of a given field. For example, he cites Charles Darwin's study of birds. Darwin had no background in ornithology, but his observational, non-scientific study of various bird species in the Galápagos Islands led to innovation. When Darwin returned from his trip, he handed over his notes to a renowned ornithologist, John Gould, who initially dismissed Darwin's findings as nothing extraordinary. Gould would later find that each of the species that Darwin had studied was indeed a unique and distinct from another. Johansson used this example to illustrate how someone from outside an industry can help move thought forward and spark innovation. Johansson capitalized on the success of the book to found the Medici Group, a consultancy firm that encourages innovation through diversity.

I have seen the Medici Effect play out in real life. If you recall, my Pegasys team at Hoffman-LaRoche had very little experience in marketing, but it had incredible diversity amongst team members. This team was a perfect example of The Medici Effect in action. The team had people from Spain, Cuba, South Africa, Kenya, Uganda, Kenya, China, Armenia, Israel, Turkey, Greece, and Lebanon. It was truly a United Nations team in terms of its diverse make-up. Based on the lack of marketing experience on that team, no one would have ever placed a bet on them succeeding in launching a brand new product for the company. Yet, in six months, they had not only launched the product, but they had also taken over market leadership. The success of the team was directly attributable to its diversity, which allowed for new ideas on how to uniquely position the product in innovative ways.

As I mentioned, that dream team was in pharmaceuticals, where I have spent most of my career. One of the key tactics in pharmaceuticals is the ability to sample and test the products. Our product was an injectable biologic that had to be kept refrigerated, and for that reason, no one had ever sampled such a product. As the team began to brainstorm how to sample our product, we were shocked to learn that a different part of the organization had set out to convince senior management that it could never be accomplished and that the organization would take a "reputational hit." When my team made me aware of the "counter-project" within the organization, I shared the following quote with the team: "It is not the height of mountain in front of the climber that stops him, and it is the tiny pebble in the shoe."

I said to my team, "The leader of that counter-movement is the pebble. Simply take off the shoe, discard the pebble, and don't take your eye off your goal. Now let's climb that mountain. I will handle the politics."

This truly diverse team developed a way to sample our injectable biologic, and they did so in an extremely creative manner utilizing a specialty distributor who would compliantly receive the sample request from the healthcare provider and ship under temperature-controlled conditions directly to the physician's office. (This is routine today, but it was groundbreaking two decades ago.) I know the reason why my team was able to innovate around this product was because they were able to look at the issues and challenges from very different perspectives.

The process actually has some scientific and biological roots. Neuroscientists have recently discovered something called "mirror neurons," and I believe these mirror neurons help explain why non-diverse groups are not as innovative and have less ideation. Mirror neurons are responsible for brain activity that is consistent with mirroring what you see, hear, and experience around you. It is a way that the brain learns. When someone says, "Oh, show and tell," and somebody learns to do a new thing or action, the mirror neurons (which can be found in the premotor cortex of the brain) begin to fire.

Our brains are wired to absorb what's around us and mirror what the brain experiences. If everything around you (i.e., all of your experiences and information) are similar because of lack of diversity, lack of different viewpoints, and your homogenous upbringing and education, then groupthink comes into play. Everyone begins to mirror one another, which stifles new ideas and overall innovation. By having input from people who have seen, heard, tasted, smelled, and experienced different things, it becomes much harder for the brain to fall into automatic mirroring.

In general, harmony and congeniality are not good for ideation. Ideation requires the challenging of norms and history. Leading diversity research expert Lloyd Mander says, "Very high interaction within a team results in a more aligned thinking and more harmonious interaction. This is good for efficiency but not for innovation."[86] For a team focused on innovation, diversity of thoughts and perspectives is essential to ideation. Disagreements and conflict foster an environment better equipped to generate the best new ideas. This so-called "creative friction" is the foundation of many of the most innovative ideas and breakthroughs throughout history.[87] Mander further explains in detail:

> Independent sharing of ideas and opinions. Perhaps the most
> difficult to achieve in practice. Once a group member has
> gathered independent information and considered it without
> external influence, they then need to share their perspective
> candidly with the rest of the group, without modifying it.
> Unfortunately, we (feeble humans) have a natural tendency to

conform within groups and not risk embarrassing ourselves by sharing a potentially ill-founded idea. This routinely leads to independent thoughts being withheld or "watered down" so that they might be more readily accepted. The other group members then miss an opportunity to consider some new information and consequently, the potential for realizing true diversity of thought is thwarted.[88]

Another way to look at this is simple mathematics. Envision that in a meeting someone posts a challenge or question to the team. Typically, the first few ideas and thoughts that come are not the ultimate solution to the problem because they lean toward the obvious or the known. These initial ideas and suggestions are usually the product of mirror neurons. However, as the team continues to discuss the issues, each team member's brain begins to make connections to a variety of ideas based on his or her experiences, education, background, and so on. In my experience, it is usually the latter ideas that prove to be the best ideas or solutions to the challenge because those ideas reflect the fullness of the discussion and the debate. These ideas are also a result of each team member tapping into their own unique experiences to formulate an innovative thought. Mathematically it is very simple: the more ideas, the greater the chance of innovation. The more diverse sources of ideas, the greater the chance of breakthrough innovation.

Growing up in Memorial Park in West New York, New Jersey, I quickly learned the necessity of diversity to create the best new ideas. To participate, you had no choice but to play every sport that was being played with every person that happened to be out that day. As I mentioned before, the neighborhood was extremely diverse across many lines. More important than learning the skills of various sports, we had to learn the lessons of the streets. I was an honor student in school, but the greatest lessons that I learned were taught at that park.

For example, I quickly realized that in order to survive, I had to befriend many of the older kids. We'd play basketball and then, at the end of the game, the older kids would drink beer. It didn't mean that I had to drink beer (but I did have my first beer quite young.). It meant that I had to be able to accept them, play hoops with them, and understand that we were all different—and that was perfectly OK! I learned that there was a place for everyone and anyone in that park.

We even had a football team that formed in Memorial Park. The last names of the players still make me chuckle—Lopez, Gonzalez, Hernandez, etc. Who would have ever thought that a bunch of grossly undersized kids with those last names would ever be able to compete on a football field? Our first year we had eleven kids show up for the team, which meant we all had to play offense, defense, and special teams. Needless to say, we always got killed. This experience taught us that we could not quit; we also learned to help each other and how to trust our teammates who often had stronger skills in any given area. And because we all had to play every position, we had to be inclusive and listen to each other's advice when we moved to unknown position or to a position of weakness.

The exposure in Memorial Park to different friends, classmates, and environments allowed me to build an incredible network of friends that I was able to leverage in my final year in high school when I became student body president. Reflecting back on that time, there is no doubt in my mind that becoming president of the class was because of the diversity of students with whom I associated. For example, I could do integral calculus with the honors students and drink a bottle of MD 20/20 with the guys at Memorial Park after winning a giant football game. The diverse perspectives that I had learned helped me to be an effective student leader because I was able to tackle the challenges and issues that plagued the student body from all perspectives, which allowed my fellow class officers and me to come up with the best ideas and solutions.

Many professional sports teams utilize a diverse approach in their coaching rosters. The coaching unit of many professional sports teams is comprised of assistant coaches and staff from the various skills on the team. There's an offensive coach, a defensive coach, a coach that has high strategic skills, and increasingly, an assistant coach or consultant from an entirely different sport. This is because the diversity in thought is known to contribute to the most comprehensive strategy. Fortunately, it finally appears that D&I is making headway into the head coaching jobs.

On the flip side, non-diverse teams stifle innovation. In his article, "Startup Cultures: Lack of Diversity Stifles Innovation," Neil Ungerleider examines the smartphone industry and the apps developed for smartphones. According to a 2010 Nielsen study, the majority of Americans under the age of 34 who also made less than $35,000 per year all owned smartphones.[89] The great majority of those people utilized their smartphones as their primary access to the Internet. In spite of the fact that millions of Americans owned smartphones and are economically disadvantaged, the smartphone and app industry focused their attention on middle-to-upper-middle class, college-educated, and young consumers centered in the urban/suburban centers of the country. This focus effectively disregarded a substantial portion of the potential market.

The reason is simple. The programmers and tech people working in the smartphone industry develop technology and apps for people like themselves. As a result, the industry is consistently missing innovative technology, and even more, a huge share of profits by only targeting people like those in their think tank rooms. Across the board, startup cultures and communities notoriously lack diversity across the spectrum: age, gender, race, socioeconomic background, etc. The case for diversity in tech is not one just for generic political correctness; the market actually demands new ideas and innovation that can only come from a diverse team of innovators. There are very few efforts to develop apps specifically for the economically disadvantaged, older consumers, or those living outside of metropolitan centers. You can see how the entrepreneurial mindset of this (quite young) group of tech developers is missing out on an opportunity to diversify their thinking and tap into new markets.

Naturally, just having a bunch of people from diverse backgrounds in a room is not going to automatically yield new ideas and innovation. An inclusive and open environment must be fostered whereby everyone feels empowered to share their ideas and perspectives, especially if it's against the consensus of the group. Moreover, it can become difficult when a diverse team comes up with new ideas that have to be presented to a group of homogenous decision-makers. Perfect set up for the "curse of non-diverse knowledge" to kill a breakthrough idea.

I had one such experience when I tried to convince my organization to implement an innovative approach to a changing customer base in the healthcare industry. I stressed the need to address hospital groups that were consolidating and purchasing private practices in the community and creating integrated care systems. I proposed an idea that not only addressed the opportunity, but it would have significantly helped with the launch of a product that impacted both community practices and hospitals. Furthermore, this proposal would have placed the company in a position of market leadership. The idea was rejected by my boss and my peers. Simply put, they didn't understand the new market model because their collective perspectives and their individual perspectives were almost perfectly aligned—hence, no innovation.

Fast forward about three or four years later, the company's lackluster launch of that product caused many people their jobs. At that point, the company engaged an expensive consulting group to basically propose, design and help implement exactly the same innovative program that I presented to them years prior. I believe that the decision-makers didn't accept the original idea because they could not visualize where the market was going. The inability to comprehend the issue and the opportunity was due to their "likeness" and "homogeneity" compounded by the fear of challenging the non-diverse leader. This not only cost the company millions of dollars paid to the consulting firm, it may have cost hundreds of millions (or billions) in lost revenue. Over the next 18 months, it became clear to the organization that customers in the proposed "Integrated Care" segment were actually driving a significantly higher market share than customers not in that segment. By the time they implemented the new structure, other companies had already begun to implement similar systems, and today it is a cornerstone of almost any product launch.

Notwithstanding the buy-in (or lack thereof) from company executives, management is the first line of action in creating an environment that is open to new ideas from a diverse team. A manager has to be receptive to new ideas, and they must encourage as well as reward those who contribute. Leading by example opens up opportunities for others to contribute ideas that are outside of the consensus of the group based on their own unique perspective. *The One Minute Manager* says it all: you reward people publicly and you counsel privately. There's no truer place for the one-minute-manager philosophy to take root than with encouraging diverse thought. Ideally, you have a diverse group that has a leader who understands how to keep ideas flowing without being critical of the discussion. This is a perfect scenario that can optimize diverse thought.

With that said, the TRUE DIVERSITY approach must be considered to increase ideation. Let's say a company is trying to break into an emerging Latin market. To do so, they engage a group of their Latinx employees as a part of an internal focus group and think tank to ideate around how to launch into the growing Hispanic market. Latinos represent the great majority of the internal exploratory group. This is good. But what if the majority of those Latinos are Puerto Ricans born in the United States? Well, because Puerto Rico is a US territory, their view may not be as relevant to other Latin American countries like Venezuela, Mexico, or Cuba. Therefore, a team made up of a mixture of Puerto Ricans, Venezuelan, Mexican, and Costa Ricans will yield more insights and innovative approaches on how to target and talk to Hispanic customers.

My point is that one might describe the predominant Puerto Rican group as a diverse group that is well equipped to address the Hispanic market when in actuality, if you apply a TRUE DIVERSITY lens and look a little deeper, you will find that the group is actually a homogenous/non-diverse group of Latinos all raised in the American culture. You may even go deeper to discover most of the Latin representatives on the team are from New York, which makes the group even less diverse. In this example, the internal exploratory team had good Hispanic representation but the homogeneity of the Hispanics within the group may not be very helpful if the emerging market is in Mexico or Venezuela. You need someone who understands Mexican or Venezuelan culture, business practices, politics, infrastructure, hiring practices and norms to truly ideate and innovate in the new market. In conclusion, your once-seemingly diverse team is no longer so diverse from a TRUE DIVERSITY approach.

It should be clear throughout all industries that diversity on a team will lead to diversity in thought, which leads to innovative ideas. The first step is obviously hiring a truly diverse team, but the work doesn't stop there. An environment must be inclusive and open so that the diverse ideas are not only encouraged but also respected as valuable. The team must understand that its varied perspectives, beliefs, and knowledge will yield the best ideas, which is what every company seeks (or at least should seek).

CHAPTER 9:

Companies That Get It Right

**"[O]ur differences enable us to be a better team –
one that makes better decisions, drives innovation and
delivers better business results. —Mastercard®**

It's understandable that much of the conversation around diversity and inclusion can seem a bit esoteric and hard to grasp, which is why it's important to look at companies that are getting it right. The examples in this chapter have been selected based on an analysis of the companies' outward-facing profiles, reviews from employees and customers, as well as some of my personal experiences. I haven't worked at any of the five companies highlighted here, and this is just a snapshot of the companies that I believe are successful not only in messaging and approach but also in implementation.

Every year, Diversity, Inc. magazine publishes "The Diversity Inc. Top 50 Companies for Diversity" list. The list began in 2001, which was when many companies began to see the business value and opportunity in diversity programs and initiatives. The reason why this list is a great tool to evaluate diversity because it is not a "pay-for-play" list, which means that companies can't pay a fee to be included on the list. Instead, the list is composed based on corporate surveys and companies can voluntarily submit to be reviewed. In 2019, Diversity, Inc. had over 1,800 companies submit to be evaluated on the list. Each participant company receives a report card that rates its performance in the following four areas of diversity management:

1. **Talent Pipeline:** Workforce breakdown, recruitment, diameter of existing talent and structures

2. **Talent Development:** Employee resource groups, mentoring, philanthropy, movement, and fairness.

3. **Leadership Accountability:** Responsible for results, personal communications, and visibility

4. **Supplier Diversity:** Spend with companies owned by people from underrepresented groups, accountability, support[90]

Three of the five companies that are highlighted here made the Diversity, Inc. list in both 2018 and 2019: Mastercard, Marriott, and Accenture. Johnson & Johnson was on the list in 2018 but fell off in 2019, while still making an impact in Top Talent Acquisition. Finally, Publix grocery stores is a much smaller company, yet I witnessed its commitment to diversity firsthand years ago. These five companies seemingly have a top-down approach from the CEOs to the consumer, and each of them views diversity and inclusion as a primary business objective. All five are brands that are familiar and that touch various aspects of our lives.

MASTERCARD

"Every one of us has something in common: we all want to belong."[91] —Mastercard

Mastercard (#8 on the 2019 list) struck a special chord with me because of their holistic and moral approach to diversity, along with their focus on older workers. The company believes that "diversity is what drives better insights, better decisions and better products."[92] CEO Ajay Banga leads the company with a philosophy focused on decency and inclusion. "Decency" instead of the word "diversity" elevates the approach to me because it taps into a core value of the company. As a company, they strive to be decent and inclusive. I found that interesting, and I really like how the word diversity, which has unfortunately become a word that can cause negative reactions, was replaced with decency. The fact that talk of diversity in of itself causes any negative reaction is a problem, but this turn of phrase emphasizes and underscores the moral intent around diversity. We should be decent and inclusive in our business practices that reflect how we are to the world.

Banga and Mastercard also refer to DQ, replacing the word diversity with decent for "Decency Quotient." The Mastercard approach to diversity or decency is a TRUE DIVERSITY approach. The goal is not merely to meet the numbers of a pie graph, but to "create meaningful connections, inspire acceptance and cultivate a culture where we all belong."[93] Bang sums it up best (and echoes many of the theories in this book) with this one statement:

> You need to harness the collective uniqueness of those around you to widen your field of vision—to see things differently, to fail harder, to innovate, and to question everything. Widening that field of vision means widening your worldview.[94]

One area of strength at Mastercard is its focus on equal pay for equal work. The company does an assessment of all of the roles within the company to ensure that the roles are equally compensated between men and women as well as benchmarked to the external market. Almost as important, Mastercard has implemented procedures for employees to raise pay disparity concerns. They've also instituted a variety of programs to assist in the education and empowerment of future employees like Girls4Tech™, which is an educational program focused on STEM where Mastercard employees mentor pre-teen girls looking toward careers in the field of digital convergence, big data, fraud detection, cryptology, and more. This overarching commitment focuses on connection and cultivation, all of which are vital in a TRUE DIVERSITY initiative. In its messaging, Mastercard uses language that promotes inclusion in a way that makes it a centerpiece of its efforts. Moreover, the fact that they tailor their D&I programs to each respective region signals that they are implementing a TRUE DIVERSITY approach. "Mastercard has been on an inclusion journey for many years. In 2018, we set a course for evolving this journey into one that is even more engaging, impactful, and for the first time, localized to each region," says Randall Tucker, Chief Inclusion Officer (note the title).

Let's close on a seemingly small practice of the company that emphasizes its big commitment to diversity and inclusion. When you receive a calendar invite for a meeting at Mastercard, the following statement is in the notes, "Have you invited colleagues who may have diverse perspectives to your meeting? This helps spark innovation and reflects our culture of belonging." The fact that the company puts that in the calendar invite for every meeting says it all.

MARRIOTT

Marriott is one of my favorite companies in general, but also for diversity and inclusion. In 2019, it ranked No. 2 on Diversity, Inc.'s list and has consistently been an innovator in the space of D&I. It was also named as one of the best multinational places to work by the employment website, "Great Place to Work."[95] In addition to these two lists, it consistently is ranked by other magazines, journals, and organizations as a leader in employment initiatives across the board.

As it pertains to D&I, the success is directly connected to Marriott's commitment to creating an inclusive guest experience for their workforce and the world. I found that interesting because they apply the inclusive guest experience not only to the guest renting the room, but also to their workforce. As we have discussed, a TRUE DIVERSITY approach is a consumer-centered business decision. Marriott's inclusion of their workforce in that consideration elevates the impact overall. As one of the first companies to adopt an integrated D&I program over 25 years ago, Marriott's philosophy is that "success is never final" and the company is always looking for ways to improve the experience for its workforce with a focus on the guests.

One of the unique ways Marriott approaches D&I is by "pushing decision-making down."[96] By pushing decision-making down, you're creating an inclusive culture by default. For example, if you're at the Marriott in uptown New York City, then the ethnic, racial, cultural, and socio-economic background is going to be different than a Marriott in the middle of Iowa (or even in the middle of Times Square, for that matter). By pushing decision-making down, you're empowering the Marriott employees (who will likely have a more diverse workforce) to make decisions directly.

I believe this fosters inclusion because employees don't have to pick up the phone to call a corporate office outside of the area that has no hands-on knowledge about the guests that frequent the hotel. To me, this becomes an inclusion strategy because the company is compelled to turn to onsite employees for decision-making and policy feedback. Notwithstanding outliers, I think it also alleviates employee bias in direct decision-making because there is no corporate scapegoat or policy for biased decisions. The employee has ownership of their decisions and the outcome, either positive or negative.

From a D&I programmatic perspective, Marriott is also leading the way. With its Serve 360 program, Marriott develops programs and partnerships that develop skills and opportunities in hospitality for people from underrepresented groups such as minorities, women, people with disabilities, veterans, and refugees. It has pledged to spend $5 million to deepen the reach and impact of these programs in the hopes of developing additional skill sets to increase the access to a diverse workforce across the entire hospitality industry.

Marriott's Culture Days provides employees an opportunity to share their cultures and immerse themselves in the diverse cultures of their fellow employees. The program is a key to building cultural competency and knowledge for their workforce, which ultimately increases the capacity for empathy amongst diverse employees. Understanding the cultural background of your co-worker leads to the reduction of bias and insensitivity in the workplace.

The Emerging Leader's Program (ELP) focuses on increasing the number of women and minorities in leadership positions in the company. As previously discussed, if you look at the pie graph and see that your percentages look diverse, but then on closer inspection discover that most of the women and minorities in your organization are in low or entry-level positions, then your organization is not truly diverse. Marriott's ELP program is designed to train and promote women and minorities into leadership roles. According to Marriott's internal data, "More than 1,300 leaders have completed or are currently enrolled in this program. Overall, women have represented 56% of participants and minorities have represented 36%. Since the program's inception in 2014, 60% of participants have been promoted at least once."[97] As a result of Marriott's focus on promoting women and minorities through the ELP, the company was able to make a substantial impact on the number of minorities and women in leadership roles. It's a great example of a company applying a TRUE DIVERSITY approach by ensuring that the company is diverse at all levels, particularly at the management and senior management levels.

ACCENTURE

Accenture's CEO, Julie Sweet, has set the bold goal of becoming the most diverse company in the world, and the company is aggressively implementing strategies to achieve it. At No. 7 on Diversity Inc.'s list, Accenture is a great company for women, who make up more than 42 percent of its global workforce. The company also boasts a robust employee resource group ("ERG") for women with over 6,000 members in the United States, and the group provides "a range of networking opportunities to aid career advancement, work/life balance, recruiting, external relations, and community access."[98] The company has also set the goal of increasing the number in its United States workforce to 40 percent by 2020, and it plans to achieve a gender-balanced workforce by 2025. A key aspect of its plan that I believe will have a great impact is its commitment to increase the percentage of female managing directors to 25 percent by 2020. Women account for 47 percent of Accenture's new hires.

In addition to its strong focus on gender parity in its workforce, Accenture also fosters an accepting and inclusive environment for its LGBT employees. With over 45 Pride Networks across the globe, Accenture is one of the most inclusive global companies when it comes to celebrating the diversity of the orientations of the workforce. Accenture also boasts an LGBT ally network of over 100,000 allies a number, which has grown five-fold since 2017.

One of the programs that will have an impact beyond its workforce and customer base is Accenture's Diverse Supplier Development Program ("DSDP"). The DSDP is a training program for "protégé" business that lasts between 12 to 18 months where business owners from diverse backgrounds are paired with senior executives to help grow and improve their businesses. On the company website, Accenture explains that: "The goal is to pair DSDP protégés with Accenture executive mentors in their industry who can provide more-targeted, experience-based guidance."[99] This undoubtedly has a trickle-down and outward effect as these businesses grow and employ more diverse populations. It is the way to build diversity at all levels of business interaction—not just within the workforce, but also in the supplier base.

Accenture also celebrates diversity internally. The company hosts the annual "Inclusion & Diversity Excellence Awards" that provides recognition for the company programs, initiatives, and leaders that are making significant and innovative impact on the company's diversity strategy. The awards are employee-driven with employee votes determining the global winners.

It is clear Accenture aims to be a leader in diversity, as demonstrated in the study, "Getting to Equal 2019: Creating a Culture that Drives Innovation." The company conducted "the first research in the marketplace to prove that a workplace culture of equality is a powerful multiplier of innovation and growth."[100] I have used many of the critical findings from the study throughout this book. Finally, Accenture has joined several business organizations and resolutions that focus on diversity and inclusion, including the Business Statement on Transgender Equality,[101] the Employers for Pay Equity Pay Pledge,[102] and Paradigm for Parity.[103].

JOHNSON & JOHNSON

After working in the pharmaceutical industry for the great majority of my career, I have had a front-row seat to companies that get it right and companies that fail miserably. My favorite Pharma company from a diversity point of view is Johnson & Johnson ("J&J"). Their D&I focus is driven from the top by CEO Alex Gorsky. He connects the company's credo and vision directly to diversity and inclusion. Gorsky states, "Diversity & Inclusion at Johnson & Johnson is not just a commitment—it is the reality of how we live and work. The best innovations can only come if our people reflect the world's full diversity of individuals, opinions and approaches." And he has walked the walk when it comes to promoting Blacks and Latinos at J&J. Under his leadership, the company has tripled the rate at which it promotes minority employees.

Once again, it is because with Gorsky's leadership views D&I as a business-driven necessity. It's not some pie-in-the-sky ideal that is meant to satisfy a desire to be politically correct; it is directly related to innovation and maintaining a strong competitive advantage. The company clearly states that the focus on D&I is about "[m]aximizing the global power of diversity and inclusion to drive business results and sustaining competitive advantage." Right up front, they specifically say their purpose is to drive results and to have a competitive advantage. The company makes D&I a way of doing business, not an afterthought or a secondary consideration. It is primary to their success and how they maintain (and grow) market share.

To that end, I believe J&J has one of the best D&I statements that effectively focuses on inclusion and individuality:

> Diversity at Johnson & Johnson is about your unique perspective. It's about you, your colleagues and the world we care for—all backgrounds, beliefs and the entire range of human experience—coming together. You view the world from a unique vantage point; a perspective that gives you problem-solving potential ideas, solutions & strategies that, when mobilized, can bring health to billions.

> Inclusion at Johnson & Johnson is about creating a deep sense of belonging. It's about a culture where you are valued, your ideas are heard and you advance this culture for everyone.

> Diversity & Inclusion at Johnson & Johnson means -
> You Belong. Be Yourself, Change the World.[104]

In 2018, J&J was No. 1 on Diversity, Inc.'s Top 50 list, but it failed to make the Top 50 in 2019. It's an indication that D&I is a dynamic business consideration and it takes ongoing innovation in the area to maintain the pace. There is no direct or clear explanation of why J&J fell off the list after being #1 in 2018. It has continued many of the great programs that put it on top in the first place. More importantly, it has maintained D&I as a core of the company credo, which was revised for the company's 75th anniversary whereby D&I was made the *responsibility* of all employees.

Gorsky and all J&J executives are required to participate in a mentorship and sponsorship program, which has been accredited for 100% retention of the participants in the program. Many of those participants go on to be promoted to the vice president level within the company. According to Diversity, Inc., "[o]ver 100,000 employees globally have completed unconscious bias training and the company continues to mitigate bias in their performance standards as well as their interview, onboarding, and development processes."[105]

J&J is a great example of how important C-Suite commitment is to a successful D&I strategy. Led by Gorsky and the Chief Diversity & Inclusion Officer, Wanda Bryant Hope, the company has made D&I a business-focused objective not only to improve the numbers in a pie graph, but to utilize diversity for innovation, improved market share, and competitive advantage. The focus is on building a workforce that reflects the diversity of the company's consumers, and this top-down approach forces executives and management to look at D&I as a critical and essential component of their job. It is a True Diversity approach that landed J&J in the Diversity, Inc. top spot and Hall of Fame.

One smaller company that I want to highlight is Publix. The aforementioned companies are Fortune 200 global companies, which may make it easier or harder for them to effectively implement D&I depending on how you look at strategy. If you're not familiar, Publix is a supermarket chain located in Florida, Georgia, Alabama, Tennessee, South Caroline, North Carolina, and Virginia. When I was living in Florida, I had the option of going to multiple grocery stores, but I only went to Publix, and it was solely because of how I experienced their D&I strategy at the consumer level.

Recently, I was reading about how Publix bills itself as the place "where shopping is a pleasure." The store is almost always at the top of customer satisfaction reviews, including the American Customer Satisfaction Index, Market Force's annual customer survey, and Consumer Reports' investigations into the grocery sector. It is also the world's largesse employee-owned company, which may account for the fact that the company has not had to lay off one single employee since it was founded over 80 years ago. Employees receive stock, which probably explains why the employees have been voted the happiest in the supermarket industry. The current CEO even started out as a Publix bagger.

All of those are great facts about Publix, but as I said, I am including it in this chapter because of my personal experience as a customer. As I mentioned earlier in the book, I lived in Florida for ten years, and it was very first time I had seen employees with disabilities working in the grocery store. Keep in mind this was nearly 30 years ago, and this was not a common practice as it is now. If you don't understand the significance of the time and the importance of the job, remember that the current CEO of Publix, Todd Jones, began his career as a bagger and store clerk. In addition to employing people living with physical, mental, and developmental disabilities, the company had a no-tipping policy. Both were a part of their culture because the company believed that the customer experience was its primary focus, and taking care of its employees aided the overall experience. It was the very first time that I saw any of that in a market.

Today, a lot of supermarkets employ people living with disabilities as a form of diversity and inclusion, but Publix was doing this practice three decades ago. The proof is in the way employees consistently rank the company. Publix employees say that it's a great place to work, with the company ranking above 90% in employee satisfaction most years. This employee satisfaction spills over into the customer experience, which I can confirm I felt every time I went into a Publix. I agree with the customers who rate Publix's service in the 95th percentile for excellence. More importantly, 94% of Publix customers say they love the way the company contributes to the community, and the same percentage say that they feel welcomed when they are shopping.

If you look at the awards they have won for diversity, it further underscores my assertion that D&I drives the consumer experience. In 2017 and 2018, Publix won awards for best places to work for diversity, so of course people feel comfortable when they walk into a Publix because they see people that are like them working there. This is a way of tying the diversity movement within Publix to how their feel about shopping there. The company has also been named one of the "Best Places to Work for Parents,"[106] amongst other key indicators that improve D&I. Basically, no matter how you peel this onion, Publix is addressing diversity from a lot of different angles.

With all of the great initiatives and progress these companies have made; it is clear there is no perfect company because there are no perfect people. However, these companies have made a valiant effort to effectively create a strategic D&I plan, and they have all come out successful. The common thread amongst all of these companies is that the TRUE DIVERSITY approach to D&I is a business decision that provides for innovation and competitive advantage driven by the needs of the consumer. Moreover, each of these companies understands that diversity isn't just Black and White or female and male, but a myriad of factors that contribute to ensuring that your workforce is truly diverse in thought, background, and experience all the while representing the diverse profiles of your customers.

CHAPTER 10:

Avoiding & Navigating Diversity Fatigue

"Diversity is about all of us, and about us having to figure out how to walk through this world together."
—Jacqueline Woodson

As we've seen many times throughout the book, "diversity fatigue" often comes when we discuss or research diversity and inclusion. The term first emerged in the 1990s when equal opportunity became a major initiative among major corporations and organizations. Then and now, diversity is generally seen as a positive thing, and the effort to create more diverse workforces was lauded both internally and externally. That being said, the act of doing is oftentimes exhausting and difficult work. "Diversity fatigue" described the stress that managers felt when tasked with realizing these goals.[107] Since the 1990s, the term has been used more widely (and many times inappropriately) to indicate the pushback that occurs when people believe the term is overused or the initiatives are useless public relations lip service.

This situation presents a real dilemma for anyone attempting to put forward diversity and inclusion programs or further the well-established business case for it. On the one hand, there is irrefutable data that diverse companies outperform non-diverse companies. On the other hand, the data suggests that most diversity programs do not work. The latter is a direct cause of the so-called diversity fatigue that many people experience and talk about within companies. There are ways to avoid the Catch-22 that diversity and inclusion programming presents, however. And companies need to be intentional about doing so.

Let me step back and try to explain what I have seen and experienced as a minority employee, manager, and leader. First, traditional programs can cause resentment and trigger biases instead of helping. On multiple occasions, some of my peers (at all levels within the organizational structure) have told me that they really dislike mandatory diversity programs. From some of my peers, I understood their resentment because the programs were not designed for people like them. Many of my peers who complained were amongst the most diverse-minded leaders I have met. Their complaints about the programming stemmed from their beliefs that they were far ahead of the curve; they believed the programs were designed for the "non-diverse" manager, which made them feel inadequate, unrecognized, and guilty by association.

Secondly, most traditional programs are internally focused and pie-graph driven. The programs often start with an internal analysis of diversity within the organization, usually led by HR. The results are multiple pie graphs and linear charts to illustrate the rise and fall in the representation of various underrepresented groups. This analysis is usually confined to race and gender by organizational level. Then, external benchmarks are used to see how the organization measures up to "like" companies. Some companies purchase this data from external sources and prepare their own reports. The smarter companies use organizations such as Diversity, Inc. to give them a much broader look at diversity.

Notwithstanding this flawed approach to diversity training, the biggest failure of most companies' initiatives is the selection and implementation of training programs. Attention is not paid to tailor programs to fit the company or its specific needs. Instead, consultants or trainers are hired to present programs that are cookie-cutter and have been recycled amongst various companies across different industries. Employees can smell this approach, and it comes off as an inauthentic way to address diversity. It does not encourage or inspire employees to engage in the programming in a meaningful way, which ultimately leads to the failure of the programming to meet its objectives. As long as organizations continue to push "off-the-shelf" diversity training programs down employees' throats (literally making the diversity case "black and white"), they will continue to miss the mark and not harness the power of TRUE DIVERSITY.

An organization can avoid and/or navigate diversity fatigue by adhering to five simple rules. If you feel like you're approaching a diversity fatigue roadblock, or if you have already hit it, then you should consider implementing these tools to course correct. If you're designing new programming, then it's the perfect time to evaluate your program planning from the lens of these five components.

1. Be Proactive and Not Reactive

There is a collective eye roll when a company has a diversity, bias, or discrimination issue and then forces employees to participate in an "all-day" diversity training program. It screams inauthenticity because it's a reaction to a misstep or failure that exposes the company to potential liability. Most employees know this, and consumers do, too. Had the event not occurred, the company would not have implemented the programming, so it ultimately becomes ineffective in training employees or convincing anyone that the company is serious about diversity and inclusion.

Instead, a diversity initiative that is proactive and directly from the top leadership of a company is viewed far more favorably than one that is merely a reaction to a bad event. As we have discussed, management and employees know when the C-Suite is serious about diversity and inclusion because it is initiated, implemented, and consistently reinforced from the very top of the organizational food chain. On the other hand, an e-mail requiring employees to participate in "mandatory training" once or twice per year will inevitably create feelings of fatigue. Conversely, an ongoing effort pushed and fully supported by the most senior executives likely will be viewed as a company-wide commitment that inspires employees to have more authentic buy-in and participation.

It should also be noted that the mere existence of a senior diversity and inclusion officer does not prove a company's commitment to D&I. In far too many companies, the Chief Diversity Officer or similar title is a figurehead in place for public relations purposes with no real power to design and implement effective programming. Unfortunately, it is often the sole role in the C-Suite of many companies held by a woman or a person of color. Once again, managers and employees know when a company puts power behind this position and underscores its commitment to a truly diverse and inclusive workforce.

A TRUE DIVERSITY approach stems from a company's desire to better serve its consumer and increase its market share. It should be a business-based decision. The best of which are made from a proactive position and not one of reaction.

2. Emphasize Diversity Benefits

I don't mind sounding like a broken record by reinforcing the premise that diversity is good for business, and that fact should be the lead-off when talking about diversity initiatives. Companies are in business to make money. It is a universal principle understood from the bottom to the top of an organization. It is also generally understood that the better the company performs; the better employees will be compensated (theoretically). Even if that is not the case, everyone wants to be a part of a winning team. Diversity initiatives should be a consumer-focused business decision; then the benefits are easily identifiable and understandable.

When leadership focuses on the benefits of a diverse workforce as its sole motivator in implementing initiatives, programs, and training, it is less likely to be viewed as punitive and less likely to result in fatigue. Connecting diversity to the bottom line directly links the company's efforts to an employee's job and responsibility.

Beyond the bottom line, I believe some time and attention should be spent on educating managers and employees about the other benefits of having a diverse workforce such as innovation, increased morale, and retention of talent. As we know, all of these benefits link back to the bottom line, but for many employees, the singular consideration of profits is not enough motivation to inspire them, nor is it enough to prevent diversity fatigue.

3. Be Innovative and Intentional With Programming

As I mentioned, most diversity training is ineffective. The primary reason is that they are cookie-cutter or off-the-shelf programs that are not tailored to your company's specific needs, customers, or employees. Frankly, most programs and training are boring, redundant, and lack creativity. In this day of diversity-and-inclusion overload, being innovative is a great way to ensure that the programs are effective and impactful. No one wants to sit through another mandatory seminar with some "expert" talking about diversity. Moreover, most programs don't achieve the thing most required for individual change, which is building or increasing empathy.

According to Audrey Gallien, a Senior Director in Catalyst's Learning and Advisory Services, "We see fatigue when companies do not invest in the skill sets of vulnerability and connection that are required to understand the intrinsic benefit of increasing diversity. Without the skill of connecting across difference, something that the *majority of our population* has never been taught, people can hide behind silence, resistance, and frustration in deep misunderstanding."[108] Programs that focus on action rather than awareness are far more successful in helping to build the interpersonal tools needed to implement TRUE DIVERSITY programming. At varying degrees, everyone is aware that bias and discrimination exist, but a program that inspires an employee to examine their own biases and then take action is far more effective than a "talking head" seminar from an expert.

Leaders from some of the companies in the previous chapter have implemented innovative programming to aid their diversity and inclusion initiatives. Some of these include the use of entertainment resources such as film and television, interactive role-playing training, and cultural exchanges, all of which have helped employees from diverse backgrounds see the benefits of having various perspectives on a team and in the workforce. More importantly, these types of innovative programs are fun, entertaining, and far more likely to hold the employees' attention.

In addition to being innovative in approach, a TRUE DIVERSITY program should also be intentional and specific to a company's workforce. Therefore, when leaders are looking for programs and trainings, they should actively look for programs that are suited to their workforce and then further tailor those programs so that the program is not arbitrary or inauthentic to its audience. Once again, this takes more focus and work, but if the goal is to implement programming that is effective, then it will be worth the additional effort.

4. Rename Programming

Here is a simple and short point with the potential to have a great deal of impact: change the name of the company's programming. The words diversity, inclusion, bias, mandatory, and training have become triggers for so many of us. Employees immediately place these words in the "undesirable" file of their brains whenever they crop up in a company-wide e-mail or newsletter. A little creativity will go a long way here.

By simply changing the name of the programming, you can remove the negative triggers that have unfortunately become associated with diversity and inclusion. Integration, belonging, cultural exchange, workforce, or innovation are just a few words that might be more effective when naming programming.

5. Highlight Successes

If your company has enjoyed great successes (or even just modest success in its efforts), don't be quiet about it. Celebrate and publicize the successes internally. People like to know that their efforts and participation have not been in vain. Create programs that reward and award managers and employees who have excellent track records that go beyond just the slices of a pie graph. By highlighting and celebrating the people and teams that are getting it right, it inspires and encourages others within the company to do the same. There is nothing more motivating than healthy competition. And it wouldn't hurt if there were compensation or some other desirable perks directly connected to high performance in the areas of diversity and inclusion.

It's also helpful to put a spotlight on employees and teams that are leading innovation from within the company. By sharing their successes and accomplishments, it will undoubtedly spark ideas and innovation from others. At the same time, the sharing of ideas moves the company toward utilizing the best practices company-wide. It's a win-win situation that allows employees to receive recognition for their commitment and work while motivating other employees to do the same.

A great idea is to design a competitive program that shows the benefits of having a diverse team. We should start with the questions; can diverse teams out-perform non-diverse teams? Then create the teams and ask them to tackle a project. Finally, measure the outputs of the teams and report it to the organization at large.

The key to this challenge is to ensure that the skill sets within the teams are equalized. This type of challenge relates directly to work productivity and will hopefully not be viewed as an "off-the-shelf" diversity program.

Overall, if you don't want diversity and inclusion to become a lame initiative, and if you want your employees to avoid diversity fatigue, then you must 1) position diversity and inclusion as a positive tool for exceptional business performance and 2) avoid using diversity and inclusion as a punitive tool for non-diverse managers. Be proactive. Be innovative. Be creative. Be congratulatory. Be committed to a TRUE DIVERSITY approach.

CLOSING NOTE

I want to go back and revisit a statement that I made earlier in the book. As a young man, I heard the sentence, "A nosotros nos mastican pero no nos tragan" ("They will chew on us but not swallow.") It is our responsibility, and no one else's, to make people swallow. Swallow means to internalize diverse viewpoints, to allow us to make them better. How we do that is by becoming the very best at whatever we choose to do. If we become:

- a great neurosurgeon like Dr. Benjamin Carson, every hospital system will want you to operate on their patients;

- a great military leader like Colin Powell, everyone will want you to lead them in times of peace or war;

- a great chef like Jose Andres, everyone will want to dine at your restaurant;

- a great architect like Isabel Castilla, everyone will want you to design their version of the NY High Line.

Being different is your advantage. There are many people out there who understand this and want to integrate your talents into their businesses. Find those people and those companies. And run like heck from those who simply see you as a statistic on a pie graph. It is those who will one day become a statistic in the book of failed businesses.

True Diversity Conversations

A True Diversity Conversation With
Antonious Porch, Esq.
General Counsel, SoundCloud

TRUE DIVERSITY: Please tell us your hometown, education, occupation, current role and any other identifiers that you think are relevant to who you are.

ANTONIOUS: I grew up in Chicago and was fortunate enough to be able to go to the East Coast for college. I went to Yale undergrad and studied psychology and was super active in the community in part through the radio station that I ran, which was a commercial radio station. It was a great experience.

As part of my studies in psychology, I focused on advertising—its impact and ability to influence. Additionally, the ability of advertising to deliver a message and, ultimately, to connect with people. At the radio station, I also had the fortunate opportunity to bridge the college campus that was Yale with the greater New Haven community.

Therefore, I feel like that the notion of community really tied through both my social experience and my academic studies. After graduating from Yale, I was accepted to Columbia University for law school and came to New York because I knew I wanted to focus on media.

During the bridge summer between college and law school, I worked at ABC, the television network, and was part of a program sponsored by the International Radio and Television Society Foundation. It was just this great opportunity to work in a quasi-legal role looking once again at commercials, content and the messages being delivered to consumers, to ensure that they met certain baseline standards and practices.

I then went to Columbia Law School. It cemented my interest in the intersection of media and the law. During law school, I worked part-time at a media think tank that was focused on journalism, First Amendment rights, and the freedom of the press, which really helped round out my experience.

I ended up moving back to Chicago to work at a top corporate law firm. Eventually I moved back to New York to focus on working for technology companies and start-ups by doing their corporate work and their technology transactions, including software licensing.

Over the years, I've come to focus on tech. Currently, I'm the general counsel of SoundCloud, the world's largest open audio platform, meaning anyone in the world at any time can be in his or her bedroom and upload a track to share it with the world. At SoundCloud, we focus on empowering people to connect and share through music.

It's a fantastic company headquartered in Berlin, founded by two Swedes who ended up in Germany, and I work principally in the New York Office. In my role as chief legal officer, I oversee every facet of our business that impacts our corporate structure, our intellectual property, and our brand—and ultimately, how our consumers, our listener and creator community, view SoundCloud.

I'm a black man. I'm openly gay. Frankly, being black and openly gay in technology is a really unique place to be, and SoundCloud is a fantastic fit for me and my identity because it allows me to marry my values with the focus on global inclusion and diversity within my day-to-day work. The audience SoundCloud serves are young listeners and creators who are heavily involved in EDM and hip-hop, and an audience that's largely African-Americans, Asian-Americans, and Latinos. Internally, as a member of the executive team, I serve as the executive sponsor of our Clouds of Color, which is our employee resource group for people of color, employees, and our allies.

TRUE DIVERSITY: Being black and openly gay, it would seem that the impact of that has changed over the course of your career. Can you talk about that a little bit?

ANTONIOUS: Well, I came out during college, and when I was applying to law school, I intended on being openly gay. I think that was another reason I was drawn to New York. It felt like a place that could accommodate my identity and my openness while also fueling my professional and personal interests in things like music and culture.

Then, when I thought about where I might start my career, I actually focused on California firms because at the time that I was in law school, there were not a lot of firms that openly and actively recruited LGBT law students or who had prominent LGBT attorneys in their ranks.

The firm where I spent my summer—sort of a pivotal summer between second and third year—was Morrison & Foerster, which was a San Francisco-based firm. At the time, Morrison & Foerster became the first law firm to have an openly gay chairman, which was huge for a firm of its size and caliber.

I had such a great experience there that I decided to join another California firm, Latham and Watkins, when I moved home to Chicago because again it felt like the California values and accommodation for diversity being both a person of color and also openly gay was unique in the legal profession. Over time, that has totally changed.

I think in some respects, at least on the LGBT front, it has become somewhat unremarkable to be openly gay as a law student and seeking out a firm. Many of the firms, especially the more prominent firms, seemingly have come a long way and have openly gay partners and openly gay senior associates, which is great.

I still think in terms of being African-American, that was its own unique challenge. Long before someone would necessarily find out that I was gay, they could see clearly that I was African-American, and the truth is as an African-American, you walk into a room or a meeting unfortunately with some question marks or some gaps that have to be filled that have nothing to do with you as an individual. But, it's everything about your identity.

I won't quite say there's a dark cloud over your head, but there is this questioning by your superiors, colleagues, and clients. Who am I really dealing with and who am I working with? And I think some of those challenges, which are cultural, are still in play for African-American law students and African-American lawyers.

Although there are certainly many more black partners in major law firms, I don't think there are enough and I frankly don't think that law firms have advanced quite as far as they want with respect to hiring and retaining African-Americans and Latinos within their ranks. So, there's definitely work to be done.

With that said, certainly it is better today than when I started. At SoundCloud, one of the things I do as a general counsel—because I'm in a position to do this—is I focus on recruiting and retaining a diverse staff and team. I actively look for female lawyers and people of color and bring them into the organization. Then, I do the next, and often more important, step of nurturing and supporting them in their careers.

When selecting and managing the outside law firms and counsel we hire, I also raise the questions: 1) "How will you staff the work for us? and 2) What is the firm doing in regard to diversity within its own ranks? That becomes important, and the firms that I work with tend to have at least diversity in scope and seem to be making strides in diversity whether or not diverse lawyers are on my matters. But increasingly diverse attorneys are in fact working on the deals and the matters of our outside firms.

TRUE DIVERSITY: What does the word "diversity" mean to you?

ANTONIOUS: Diversity is visible representation and openness to people who are not the same—and, let's be clear, those differences come in lots of colors and flavors. So, for me, it's looking around the room and seeing a New York City subway-like representation in terms of shades, hues, ethnic backgrounds, gender, gender identities, and sexual orientation.

Being at SoundCloud has really hammered that home. We have such a global presence and the types of creators we interact with are so diverse. It's impossible to think that we could set goals or Key Performance Indicators ("KPIs") for ourselves and expect to grow revenue or grow the usage of our platform and not speak to each of those differences. Internally, we also need to have access to people who have genuine connections to those differences who can speak to those communities, who can help us see how the needs and opportunities in those communities are different from other communities.

Definitely, diversity means having both that visible difference in the room with different backgrounds and different ways of thinking as well as being open to having that type of difference present.

TRUE DIVERSITY: What aspects of your background or identity that can't be found on a pie graph do you believe have been essential to your success?

ANTONIOUS: I think definitely coming from a working-class Midwestern background has afforded me the ability to retain relations and relatability with everyday folks and those who may be living on a limited budget. I think it has given me an opportunity to view our consumer engagement through that lens.

It played out when I was at Nickelodeon and we were looking at how to create content in a digital space and one of the things that we really prized was ensuring that we had a deep and broad free content experience online. Other companies were charging and you needed a credit card to access the content—you needed money to be able to have an engaging, enriching and delightful online experience.

We recognized that a lot of folks and families and kids didn't have access to a credit card. Therefore, we needed to make sure that we were creating content and experiences and leveling the playing field for fun and discovery by assuring that the content was free and accessible.

Free, ad-supported content. I think my commitment to ensuring that that sort of business model existed was very much tied to my experience growing up in a working-class household.

I'm also very spiritual. I'm a Christian, and to me, being mission-driven is part of my religious identity. So being in companies that are mission-driven, even if those missions aren't necessarily overtly or expressly Judeo-Christian, but the same sort of muscle memory around having a set of values and beliefs and ensuring that what you're doing connects to that and is reflected in that.

Back to diversity and this openness of welcoming different points of view and different looks as well as presentations in a room, at SoundCloud, it's about one common value of wanting to create a fantastic experience that lets creators and listeners connect and share their music.

It all resonates and I'm able to activate my muscle memory. That's something you wouldn't see in that sort of two-dimensional pie graph.

TRUE DIVERSITY: I love that answer, and it leads me into my next question, which is another one of our assertions or theses in the book. We believe the argument for diversity should really be a customer-based argument. It's not just a PC thing. Instead, it's really about the customer or consumer.

Can you expand on how the diversity of a team helped you understand your customer better?

ANTONIOUS: I was thinking back when I was at Nickelodeon. The FCC was working on applying some television rules around advertising and marketing to kids in the digital space, and I believe they were really trying to be thoughtful about it in the protection of children. The FCC was trying to balance the interest of regulation and the concern from children advocates with what we were saying from a business standpoint.

My team was comprised of men and women of different socio-economic backgrounds and was very racially diverse. I think that having discussions about how those different communities might engage with and access content.

Personally, coming from a black, working-class background, this notion of having access to free content that didn't require payment was important to allow access to children who did not have the means to afford a subscription fee, and it informed my stance in the discussion.

I also must admit that even hearing from others where were from more affluent backgrounds about the need to speak to parents and families who maybe see things a little bit differently and look at the enriched content in a premium model also helped me to see that there was a need to advocate for that as well.

In our work developing a proposal to the government about how to extend the TV rules to online/digital, I think we were able to come up with some ideas that balanced the needs of both types of communities and consumers and I actually think the proposal was stronger as a result of that kind of diversity around the table.

TRUE DIVERSITY: How can companies utilize the true diversity of their workforce to their advantage?

ANTONIOUS: Well, within the boundaries of the law, you start by asking people what ideas, backgrounds, and different perspectives they bring to the table. You ensure that you've got an actual structure that supports that type of engagement and dialogue. I think employee resource groups are one awesome way of doing that.

Again, you can identify the diversity and the richness of perspective and experience within the ranks. But then in a real formal way, you can tap into encouraging the elevation and awareness of the diversity within the company.

Once you do that, you begin to empower people from diverse backgrounds, and then allies who have become more aware of the presence of diversity within their ranks to begin to apply those filters in planning out a strategic business plan. Also, trying to identify pockets of consumers that you might not have otherwise considered.

After which, you can take it one step further and engage in pro-social initiatives that begin to connect your brand and your company with the values, and in some cases the heritage, associated with those communities, so that you get an authentic read into the experiences and an authentic appreciation for the history of those communities.

In theory, this approach should give you a sounder sense about how to engage and activate those communities and monetize your product or service in a way that fuels buy-in for those communities.

Again, you ensure that your culture, your stated vision, and your values are all conducive to people openly identifying the things that are beyond the visible. Then, provide them with the opportunity for structural and organizational support.

Once you've accomplished that, invite those perspectives to give voice to those perspectives in the room and make sure that you're hearing from everyone in the room who may come from those backgrounds.

Then you can begin to think about how do you outreach and do pro-social activity into those communities, so that you're having those real, true and authentic culturally relevant connections with the community—your consumers.

If you do all of those things, I feel like business benefits will undoubtedly follow. Along the way, you will have given people who helped to build the product or service an opportunity, which will allow you to deliver a more authentic product or service to existing consumers and hopefully attract new ones.

TRUE DIVERSITY: How does an organization or a team overcome the so-called diversity fatigue?

ANTONIOUS: I think there are always going to be people who don't get it, and I think you first have to acknowledge and accept that there are going to be people who don't get it.

First of all, what you have to do is continually bring in new people into a company. When you breathe new life into a company, you find new ways of engaging. I think, as with anything, if you keep doing the same old thing, the same old way, it will get old. At some point, it will have diminishing returns and won't be quite as effective as it was the first few rounds.

I also believe that by virtue of young people, new voices in the room and new seats at the table, that there will be innovation on diversity and inclusion.

At some point, you do want to get to a place where it is not just a conversation, but also a reality

It may be tiring for some and it may be challenging for others. But until we can all look around the room and feel like the room reflects the community outside, then we have to push forward and push past that.

You know, if people are struggling with that or tired, then frankly maybe some of those people don't belong in the next chapter of the company or the industry. We have to accept that too and be prepared to shift beyond those for whom it is fatiguing to shift towards that part of the mission.

Every day I get up and diversity and inclusion is what I live. Any success that I have is a reflection of the efforts of so many who came before me, and it is my obligation to continue to push forward. It is also my obligation to ensure there's more opportunity for everyone. I genuinely believe business is better when we set that out and we all commit to it by making it a part of our mission and our core values, both personally and for the organization.

Antonious Porch *is the General Counsel at SoundCloud, the world's largest open audio platform. In his role, Porch is responsible for the company's legal affairs and public policy strategy, and the management of its global team of legal experts in content licensing, copyright, data protection and privacy, and corporate matters.*

Antonious joined SoundCloud from Shazam, a London-based mobile entertainment company where he served as General Counsel. Prior to Shazam, Porch spent over a decade at global media company Viacom as Senior Vice President & Deputy General Counsel, Nickelodeon, and Vice President, Senior Counsel of Technology & Kids Compliance in Viacom's corporate office. Earlier in his career, he held roles at Classic Media (now DreamWorks Classics, part of NBCUniversal), and the law firms of Latham & Watkins and Morrison & Foerster.

A Chicago native, Antonious Porch is a graduate of Yale College and Columbia Law School and also successfully completed a cable executive management program at Harvard Business School. He serves on the board of the IRTS Foundation and lives in New York City.

A True Diversity Conversation With
Fleur Lee
Brand Lead – Unnamed Pharma Company

TRUE DIVERSITY: Please tell us your hometown, education, occupation, current role, and any other identifiers that you think are relevant to who you are.

FLEUR: I'm a 44-year-old woman who lives in Brooklyn, New York. I grew up in Chicago. I pretty much spent the years from age three to twenty-one in the Chicago city limits, but then I went to school in the suburbs on the north shore of Chicago. I graduated from the University of Illinois at Urbana-Champaign with a degree in medical sociology.

After graduation, I did an internship at the National Minority AIDS Council, which is relevant from a diversity perspective, and then I moved on to work in public health. I attended grad school at Columbia University where I received a master's in public health. For the greater part of my early professional career, I worked in health economics and market access at Pfizer, Inc.

I left Pfizer in 2012 to work for a biotech company helping to launch an antibiotic, and from there, I worked at various global companies, including a French company, and now I work for a Japanese company where I am based in Northern New Jersey.

I'm Asian American, specifically ethnically Chinese-American. My parents are immigrants. I'm an immigrant. I grew up with an immigrant grandmother who lived alongside us in our household. My grandmother and parents kept a lot of the Chinese traditions alive in our family.

I have two identical twin girls that are Chinese, Korean, Portuguese, and Italian. So yes, my children are of mixed race and ethnicity. In certain Asian cultures, we call them "hapa."

Even though I'm Chinese, I was born in a Southeast Asian country and I also grew up mainly in America in a very privileged north shore upbringing in the suburbs of Chicago.

TRUE DIVERSITY: Tell us about the neighborhood you grew up in when you moved to Chicago. Did being Asian in that neighborhood have any positive and negative impact on your thoughts about diversity?

FLEUR: Until kindergarten, I grew up on the north side of Chicago in Lake View. After kindergarten, we moved to a suburb of Chicago called Skokie, which is really interesting because it was predominantly Jewish at the time. There were probably three Asian families that I knew of in grade school. Everybody else was pretty much of Jewish decent, and then for high school, we ended up moving back to the Chicago area. Although we'd moved back into the city, I went to an Irish Catholic high school on the north shore in a suburb, Wilmette, where everyone was pretty much Irish Catholic. They were either Filipino or Irish Catholic, blonde and blue-eyed.

It was a very interesting shift from being in a predominantly Jewish community to a privileged, affluent white Irish community for high school.

TRUE DIVERSITY: What does the term diversity mean to you?

FLEUR: Well, diversity means a mixture of people in an environment where there are people of different genders, ethnicities, races, religious backgrounds, and sexual orientations. To me, diversity means a very representative sample or environment that reflects what the world looks like, including ethnicity, race, gender, sexuality, religion, and age.

TRUE DIVERSITY: In terms of those identifiers of your background—being an immigrant, Chinese-American, etc.—can you attribute any of them as having been critical to your success?

FLEUR: I'm really interested in intersectional identities and politics, and I think what I have always thought about and very strongly identified is the fact that I am Asian-American, but also very much an immigrant. My family moved from China to Burma (which is now Myanmar) then to the US.

Basically, my parents started over in each of those countries, and I think the American ideal of pulling yourself up by your bootstraps was instilled in me from an early age. Although I grew up in America, I primarily identify as an immigrant who has been able to follow in the footsteps of my parents, both of whom worked very hard, sacrificed, and ultimately were successful in several countries.

My mom taught me very early that your education is the one thing that you can always take with you. She taught me that when borders, the environment, or economics strip you of your wealth, the only thing you can take with you is your mind, which includes all of your knowledge and education. Because of those lessons, I always knew I was destined for greater education and I knew education was a gateway to opportunities. In fact, those opportunities would put me in a position where I could be a decision-maker, an influencer and, most importantly, have great impact in the world as well as in my life.

TRUE DIVERSITY: We know that companies often look to pie-graph indicators and make determinations that the company does not have enough Asian women, for example. How does your background differ from other women who might check those two boxes?

FLEUR: Growing up Chinese was a very strong piece of my identity. But being Chinese is a very interesting and complex titling or identity to subscribe to because, oftentimes, if you don't speak the language fluently or if you didn't grow up in Mainland China, you are not considered technically Chinese. You're seen as tainted in some ways by other Chinese.

Because I grew up in America, I'm often not considered Chinese by the standards of native-speaking Chinese people. If you were Chinese but born in Vietnam, they wouldn't necessarily consider you Chinese.

It's very interesting growing up in that environment knowing that I was Chinese, but there was just always like underlying subtext that I wasn't *really* Chinese.

Being born in a Southeast Asian country, Burma, also makes me unique as Chinese. It's seen as being 'exotic' to have my background of where I was born and grew up as a child.

Personally, I am Chinese-American, but I have a very diverse group of friends. Oftentimes people will come to a party that I will host and they are always surprised at the range of diversity at my parties. I've got some Asian friends. I have some white friends. It's also interesting because I have a very strong East and West African connection along with a strong Latino population, and I think people are always like, "Wow, how do you know so many East and West Africans?" I think it's just the environment that I grew up in and the friends that I kept and the relationships I've cultivated.

My friends range so much in ethnicity, race, wealth, socio-economic status, and what I've always loved seeing when I have these parties is how my friend mix. They don't necessarily run in the same circles, but they are all great people doing interesting things, so they blend very well together. It is representative of how I ideally view diversity—my parties are a great representation of that across the board.

I love to see them interacting with each other, connecting and developing relationships. There's a great Bible verse, "He cuts off every branch of mine that doesn't produce fruit, and He prunes the branches that do bear fruit so they will produce even more," (John 15:2 NLT). This sums up my friends at my parties. People branch off and they grow. I love seeing the fusion and synergy that is directly connected to the diversity of my friends.

As I said, I look at intersectional politics and identity. I subscribe to that in terms of how I live my life by constantly nurturing these relationships and friendships, which have organically come to me.

TRUE DIVERSITY: How do you use that in your professional life?

FLEUR: I believe because I have a public health background and I am working in an environment where I am in service to people that it is extremely helpful. As a result, I tend to make sure there is diversity in thought and that there is an appreciation for people who are different than me.

I think diversity is a challenging subject because people who are in power are often not very diverse. If you're a person of color, you end up being in an environment where you're not even with other people that look like you or considering experiences that will help communicate to diverse communities the information or service you are marketing

It's important to be considerate of all the other people who are out there in this world and have their thoughts and their ideas represented, because growing up and not feeling represented is a disservice to your identity, your sense of entitlement, and your sense of opportunity that you feel is available to you. I mean those things are all real things that show up as consequences for environments that are lacking in diversity.

TRUE DIVERSITY: Do you have any professional examples where diversity has played a role in the success of a team? Basically, where a diverse team created a space for innovative ideas.

FLEUR: I think because I work in public health, a lot of medications that I've worked on are innovative, and the one thing that I think about as a marketer is the cross-section of social economic drivers. At its core, marketing is communication.

The focus is always on how your company or team is communicating to people so that they feel represented, have insight, and an ability to identify with what you're marketing, whether it is a product, information, or a service.

When I worked at the National Minority AIDS Council, it was important to recognize that people of different races and ethnicities were most at risk because they were not being spoken to, and I took that on there. It was a stepping-stone into working in public health.

I see the world in a way where you really need to understand how people experience things, what their culture is, so that you actually are able to have the most impact regardless if you're marketing to them to buy a product or to have public health information that will improve their diet, utilization of medication, or lifestyle changes.

All of those things are the core of what I do as a public health professional, wanting to communicate and really wanting better health outcomes in the world that we live in.

TRUE DIVERSITY: How can companies encourage and utilize the different perspectives of diversity to their advantage?

FLEUR: In a world where social media is so prevalent, one thing that people need to consider is that ethnicity, race, and gender become drivers in how people get access to information and access to health. Access or lack of access can be really detrimental in terms of the type of health outcomes that they're experiencing, eventually down the line. The reality is if you're not communicating to people in a way that speaks to them, they are missing out, which could be detrimental to their health and well-being.

As a marketer, you're communicating to people first and foremost. From a business perspective, I believe people need to be more inclusive because when you're thinking about a business and the bottom line and a top line for a company, people who are at the table and communicating to certain populations, at the end of the day, they're patients, they're consumers. They are people who are decision-makers for products, devices, and information that people are trying to promote to them.

If you are more inclusive in really thinking about how unique and diverse this world is, you are able to understand better that there are consumer segments that will have access to your product, to your information. They will use your platform and promote that information to other people. It's almost like internal marketing.

So, by really recognizing diversity and being inclusive of people and the range of people that exist, you have an opportunity to really grow your market. Truly, diversity is a bottom-line consideration, especially from a marketing perspective.

TRUE DIVERSITY: Have you experienced an environment that celebrated diversity, and if you have, how did that impact your performance, if at all?

FLEUR: When you're in an environment that's inclusive and representative of the world that you live in, you ultimately feel safe. You feel that you can identify with the people that you're working with, and those things are important to feeling that you belong. It's that sense of community and belonging that you feel when you're in an environment that is diverse.

TRUE DIVERSITY: How do we avoid so-called diversity fatigue?

FLEUR: I fear that, as it presently stands, diversity doesn't mean anything. I understand that feeling. There is a lot of lip service that seems to fuel PR functions, but not real impact.

One of my friends is a diversity director for a Fortune 500 company. According to her, it's ironic that you're sitting in these roles and then you're going to these conferences for people who are espousing diversity and there's a bunch of white women in the room who have PhDs and pedigrees. You're just sitting there thinking that diversity can mean a lot more than just race. It could mean sexual orientation. It could be religion. It could be gender. But when you think about diversity, I think a lot of people automatically go towards race as one particular characteristic.

I could see how people feel that it's a lot of lip service because I think in this current political environment that we're in, we've gone backwards. So, what did all these years of talking about and focusing on diversity get us? We can avoid the fatigue with a real focus on progress and impact. Without either, there's no point to having any of these conversations, which are extremely valuable on many levels.

Fleur Lee *currently is the brand lead for her current company, and is singlehandedly responsible for all commercial strategic and tactical decisions.*

Fleur is a passionate public health advocate for the LGS community, which is abundantly evident through her drive, passion, and overall dedication to her work. She has focused on identifying new growth opportunities to ensure that healthcare providers, patients, and caregivers can realize the full benefits of her product.

Prior to her current role leading marketing efforts at her current company, Fleur amassed over 19 years of industry experience with a unique background across many therapeutic areas. She started her career at Pfizer, working on a range of award-winning and highly recognized brands including Celebrex, Lipitor, Exubera, Caduet, Torecetrapib (CETP inhibitor), Eliquis, and Chantix, among others. Following her time at Pfizer, Fleur joined the specialty biotech company Trius Therapeutics, where she led the US commercial launch for Sivextro, an antibiotic.

Fleur has a master's degree in public health from Columbia University and a bachelor of science in sociology from the University of Illinois. Fleur has visited over 40 countries, camped in the wilderness of Africa for over a month, and consistently brings a can-do attitude and an incredible sense of humor to everything she does.

A True Diversity Conversation With
Rubén King-Shaw
Chief Strategy Officer, Steward Health Care Network

TRUE DIVERSITY: Please tell us your hometown, education, occupation, current role, and any other identifiers that you think are relevant to who you are.

RKS: I was born in Washington, D.C. and was raised in and around Washington, D.C. through high school. Now, my mom is from one of the oldest African-American families in the District of Columbia. As you might know, Washington, D.C. was built originally by rented slaves in the plantations in Maryland and Virginia. So, my mother's people go back to that time. Literally, they built the streets, the monuments, dug the channels in and around Washington, D.C. My maternal grandfather came from Warm Springs, VA in the Allegheny Mountain region of Southwestern Virginia, the descendent of those who escaped slavery prior to the Civil War.

So, I'm from one of the oldest families in the nation's capital with roots in the Virginia mountains on my mother's side. To give you a sense of the timeframe we're talking about here, Asbury United Methodists Church, one of the oldest black Methodist Church in Washington, D.C. was founded in 1836, and my great-great grandparents were in that founding congregation and we've been there ever since.

My family has a long, proud lineage of Freemasonry—Eastern Star for the women and the Masons for the men. That old guard black community used to called the "Black and Blue Bloods" because of the social cohesion and the depth of the roots of my mother's family which go back over a century in the D.C. area.

My father was a Panamanian. He was born in the Republic of Panamá. If you know anything about Panamá, the Panamá Canal was preceded by the Panamá railroad, which was built in 1850s. Like the canal, the Panamá railroad was built with immigrant labor from the

West Indies, Jamaica, and Barbados, in particular. Panamá was still a province of Colombia at that time.

My father's people go back in Panamá on his mother's side to the time of that first wave of West Indian immigrants that came in the 1850s to build the Panamá Railroad. The second wave, his father's side, came in the 1880s to build the Panamá Canal. In Spanish, the term for my people on my father's side is Afro Antillano Panameño, which in English means black Panamanians from the West Indies. It is a component of the Panamanian culture that is both Hispanic and West Indian. We all spoke in Spanish and English equally.

My hometown is in Washington, D.C., yet I am a dual citizen of US and Panamá. When we went to Panamá during my childhood, I would speak Spanish, dance calypso and salsa, climb trees, and eat mangoes. I did all of the things that Panamanian boys were doing. My brothers and I were usually shirtless for days on end. It was awesome! Then, at the end of the summer, our parents would bring us back to the United States to be Americans again.

So, I think of the Washington, D.C. area as my home town, but in my heart and my mind, Panamá was home too. We moved out to the leafy suburbs of Maryland as my father's architecture practice prospered. But Panamá has always been just as much home for me. In fact, my wife and I maintain a residence in Panamá to this very day. My wife and I share a common cultural Antillano Panameño and American heritage.

I also spent a great deal of my young adulthood in Miami where I really became my own guy, my own identity and not just somebody's son or grandson. When I started my career there, I had relationships that became family to this day and a lot of social, civic, business and political connections. I met my wife, married, and we had our two beautiful daughters there. So, Miami is as much home as Panamá and Washington, D.C. In essence, all three of those three places are my home towns depending upon the day, the minute, and what I'm doing.

I attended high school at Richard Montgomery High in suburban Maryland. I went on Cornell University where I graduated with a bachelor's of science in Industrial and Labor Relations. I then went on to get two master's degrees, one in Health Services Administration at Florida International University in Miami, and another in International Business with combination of studies at Chapman Graduate School of Business at Florida International University and in Madrid, Spain. The final chapter was the Graduate Program in Corporate Governance at the Harvard Business School.

Other identifiers that are relevant to me? I am Christian. I am a man of faith and that's a part of who I am. I identify with that as much as I do as a male and as a Panamanian, an American, a son, a husband and a father. I strongly identify with all of that.

TRUE DIVERSITY: How did your unique upbringing in both America and Panamá impact your worldview and how you show up at work?

RKS: Even as a small boy, when filling out those identifier forms, I always resented this distinction: the category that said, "black not Hispanic." It forced people like me who are Black-Hispanics to be nowhere. The ignorance that Hispanics can be black has always been a frustration and disappointment to me. Moreover, today intermixing across race and culture is more common. It is horrible to force a child to deny or prioritize one parent or one part of their cultural heritage over another.

I grew up with this sense that I am, at least in the United States of America, one of those people that nobody really either understood or nor embraced because I was outside the normal thinking patterns of American culture at the time.

It's equally true with African-Americans. At that time, nobody in school really knew that there were black Cubans or black Dominicans or black Brazilians and certainly not black Panamanians. And so, I'd get questions regularly like, "What kind of black are you?" "Are you more black or less black or different black?" My daughters have it much easier now. The Americans have learned.

This intersection of race and ethnicity has always been a part of my making. We moved into a very prosperous suburb where were one of maybe three black or brown families out there. This is the early '70s and the world was still tense around racial issues.

Well, here's this black family called the King-Shaw family that has everything else that everybody else has: the cars, house, the swim club membership, all that kind of stuff. But we are different. We had a different culture, ate different food, listened to different music. My dad spoke with an accent that our neighbors could not place. So, did I. I still do. And so, I had to learn to somehow make sense of all of that and thrive in that world and not be pulled apart. I had to learn how to be comfortable with the combination that I am. It was not easy.

As a result, from a very early age, I've learned to live with the combination of ethnicities, geographies, languages, histories. I focused a lot less on whether somebody else understood that or not. I am happy to educate and happy to connect the dots, happy to focus on what I have in common with someone because we could have a lot in common in many different ways. Yet I focus less on how we are different unless that difference is enriching to the conversation—or a barrier.

I'm a strategist in the healthcare sector and I've understood for a long, long time that healthcare is a very culturally rooted issue in many cases. Family traditions, diet, living patterns. They are part of the Social Determinants of Health outcomes. Hypertension, for example, has disproportionately high rates among African-Americans, Native Americans, and Hispanics. A lot of that is because of the diet, the customary foods and the motabulation of certain items such as salt in the physiology of African-Americans and Hispanics. African-Americans tend to retain water with salt more than others. That is essential for survival in the hot, dry regions of Western Africa, the ancestral home of most African Americans in North America.

So, there is this contribution effect of physiology, but one's culture can be an influencing factor as well. It's also understanding, frankly, that some cultures think about age differently, whether you're Anglo-American, Italian American, or African-American or Hispanic or Asian or Jewish. I have my own particular combination of cultures that I had to reconcile and live with. That made has made me very astute and sensitive to its importance for patients, families, and communities.

We can have culturally-competent healthcare services and we can provide services—social and clinical—throughout the delivery system that embraces a real patient-centered approach to care which is not just clinical, but social, cultural, and in some cases, spiritual.

TRUE DIVERSITY: How did you maintain your identity amidst the pressure to assimilate within various organizations?

RKS: By the time I started working, I had grown up in an environment where blending in wasn't really an option. Going back to my years in elementary school, moving out to Rockville, MD in 1971 was a real shock. In my elementary school, there were no Hispanics to speak of at the time. The Hispanic and West Indian culture were expressed at home, especially when our family came in from Panamá or at parties. There weren't very many West Indians close by, either. But both my parents went to Howard University, which had a very large West Indian student body. When I was in school, most of the black kids in school lived on "one side of the tracks" and I lived on the other side of the track where all the white people lived. It was extremely difficult to find acceptance in either camp in the early days.

I made the swim team shortly after we moved into one of those residential club communities. In my first year, we swam against swim club that did not want to want to let me in because I was black in this restricted club. I experienced having my white teammates rally around me and say, "If he doesn't swim, none of us do." We forced it. So, to avoid a big scandal, they let me in. Then I went in and kicked everybody's ass because, after all, I was determined to be good. I was going to be the best because I wasn't going to disappoint my teammates who stood up for me. I was nine years old.

Back then, "black people didn't swim." Basketball, football, track and field, yes. But swim team? And so, it was very hard for a lot of the black students to relate to me as a swimmer guy. So, I played basketball in my junior and senior years, and ultimately became the de facto team captain. I felt I had something to prove. I lettered in both sports.

Yet in high school I had few successes assimilating into either of those groups and being wholly accepted, which became very tiring. It got to the point that it was no longer my ambition to assimilate anymore. I didn't want to, and I didn't feel the need to do it. I focused on being good at whatever I set out to do. I figured that if I was good at enough things, the world would afford me the ability to connect socially.

Years later, in college and graduate school and throughout my career, I didn't feel the pressure to become a "cookie-cutter anything." By the time I started my career, I had dispensed with that because in my early years, I wasn't allowed to assimilate. I tried. It didn't work. And so, it became unimportant that I fit in that way.

I have my friends—some who are family to me in every way but blood—and they are very diverse and that's fantastic. Yet our friendship is not based on me being like them. It's based on bonding on the values and beliefs and experiences have in common and appreciating where we different.

TRUE DIVERSITY: As a person of color, how do you deal with the burden of representing all black people or all Hispanic people when you're the only one in the room?

RKS: Of course, I've encountered that on a daily basis. I will answer it in two ways. We were raised to have high standards and high expectations, and that starts with having high standards and expectations of myself and then high standards for others, but it starts with myself.

In every way, I want to be an example of doing it right. I say often to people, I've gotten things right. I've gotten things wrong. I've gotten more right than wrong by a pretty wide margin, but it's not that I get it right all the time. I do this no matter where I am or what I do. I do carry a certain responsibility to do and be the best I can do and be. I want that to start with a statement about Rubén.

If I come across a person who is inclined to think, "Well, black people can't do this or Hispanics can't do this ..." or whatever it is, I'm happy to be the one to say, "Well, actually, some can't. But some can. And not all white (Asian, Muslim, Jewish, etc...) people can do it either." And so, I do embrace the opportunity when I have it to open someone's eyes and say, "You are thinking about this in an outdated or narrow way. Here, I'm proof that you are wrong about (fill in the blank) and you may think of me as the exception to the rule. With more research, now that your eyes are open, maybe you will see that I'm actually not the exception. And if I am, then there are a whole bunch of exceptions are out there."

I don't feel burdened by that. I don't feel like it is a curse that I had to live with. I believe it's a natural derivative of wanting to be the best I can be. If a person has a narrow or limited view of persons of color, and if I can help their view evolve, then great. I am happy to do that and don't feel burdened by it. As I said, I am happy to educate when and where I can, if I can.

TRUE DIVERSITY: Do you think your background or identity provided you with a competitive advantage?

RKS: There have been a few cases when HMOs and accountable care networks were being put together. Overwhelmingly, there's a tendency for the planners of the delivery system to talk to whom they know. They go to the doctors who they know, those with whom they studied, or the ones that they know about from the magazines and journals that they read.

Despite the fact that the population and customer base of their target market is extremely diverse, the leadership of the healthcare industry is actually not in most cases. It's overwhelmingly white male and female. Therefore, when they're designing these networks, they aren't speaking to the Hispanic, Black, and in some areas Indian and Muslim physicians because they don't know them and don't have access to them.

The difference for me is that I will speak to everyone who represents our consumer base. I'm a member of the Boule. I'm also a Prince Hall Mason. And so, there are social organizations that connect black people, African-Americans, in ways that most white Americans know nothing about. I am also a member of a largely Hispanic fraternal organization with alumni across the country. And so, here's an example where building a provider network in a geography, you look at the population, you see how diverse it is. You must have a delivery system that's going to care for their needs. It can't be just who you know.

I derive that insight from having a multi-ethnic identity that's not just check the box or paper, but it is an authentic identity that has been lived. You just don't call somebody and say, "Hey, you're black, I'm black, let's talk about this." Or speak in Spanish as if that is all it takes to close the deal. That conversation doesn't go well. But if you have common history, common roots, common understanding, a common base of friends or perspectives and experiences that give you credibility whether you know that person or not, there's a reference base from which you start because you have this body of work that makes you credible to them in a differentiated way.

TRUE DIVERSITY: Besides the many you have already identified, are there any other important aspects of your identity that can't be found on a pie graph?

RKS: The one that I sometimes have to make clear is my faith. Faith has become such a private thing that most people who have faith don't want to share. They don't want to express it. Separation of church and state has made your faith base or whatever you believe supposedly not relevant. You don't bring it to work with you. You don't talk about it.

And so, faith is one of those things, unless you are obviously Jewish or unless you are a Muslim or Hindu in dress and custom, it goes unknown. Particularly around Anglo and African-Americans, you don't get asked the question: "What do you believe?" For me, it is an integral part of who I am. Do I broadcast it at the top of my lungs? No. But if I have my Christian radio station playing in my office, I don't turn it down to hide it. And I do ask myself throughout the day "What would Jesus do?" And I'm not afraid to pray beyond grace at the table.

TRUE DIVERSITY: How can companies encourage employees, particularly from diverse backgrounds, to show up authentically in the workplace?

RKS: A company has to encourage its senior executives to express and champion their own identity set. I use the term 'set' because most of us have multiple identities. Then, I also encourage the employees that look up to them or work for them to do the same.

I'll give you an example. When I got to the company where I work now, I had been on the board of the organization for about 12 years. The CEO and Chairman, who is Cuban-American and a dear friend, asked me to step off of the board to handle some things within the company.

The company had a young vice president, also a Cuban American with a Spanish last name, but he would introduce himself—even in his voicemails—with an English/Anglo pronunciation of what I knew was a classic Spanish last name. My full name is Rubén José King-Shaw,

Jr. So, I often get the question, "How did that happen? That's a weird combination of a name." But it makes total sense if you know my history and cultural heritage. Which I am happy to share to anyone interested.

But I would say to this young vice president, "Dude, why do you do that?" He responded "What are you talking about?" I said, "My name is Rubén José King-Shaw, Jr. If you look at my signature, you see Rubén and José and a King-Shaw Jr, and I pronounce it the way my father gave it to me. In Spanish." I said further, "My father gave me his name. I honor him by using all of it. What is it with you chopping up your name to be some Anglo dude? That's not you."

He changed his voicemail, and from that point on, he pronounced the name the way he was raised to pronounce it. But nobody had ever encouraged him to do that. Not even the Cuban-American Chairman and CEO. The young VP believed, I think, that he had to fit in. And I said, "You can be 'The Guy,' but the guy you are. Don't hide that. That's who you are."

I think if more people did that either by ethnicity or religion or race or gender, if more people said, "Be who you are. Bring it to work. It's an asset." And that "it will come in handy so don't bury it," the workplace will become both more diverse, more inclusive, and more effective. I think that's a tiny example of what leaders can do, should do, or need to do to tell others. Sometimes we need to tell that to peers too. "Man, sister, brother, stop hiding. Bring it! It's good. It adds breadth." Most of the time, if coworkers are encouraged, people just open up and there you have it.

TRUE DIVERSITY: How do we avoid diversity fatigue?

RKS: Oh wow! I guess what I would say is I don't think we avoid the fatigue. I've experienced that for some people "diversity" is an old issue. "We are beyond that," some will say. "That's identity politics and I don't care what color you are, white or purple as far as I'm concerned." And you get this very trite, "I don't see color" kind of thing. As if our identity doesn't matter. And I think that is a dismissive point of view because what you're saying is, "Who you are, where you come from, is unimportant to me. I like you or I don't like you. You do your work or you don't. But what makes you 'you' is not interesting to me." I just find that insulting and I don't appreciate it.

I do think there is a natural fatigue of dealing with an issue, which is uncomfortable for many people. I just don't think you can avoid that discomfort. I don't think you can avoid the fatigue. I think you need to build the muscle so it doesn't get tired anymore. But if there's any way to avoid the fatigue, it is to work at it. When you want to get into good shape, you run 10 minutes and then you run 15 minutes and then you run 30 minutes and then you run an hour." Meaning, you start with short, infrequent conversations and naturally build your comfort in having longer, more frequent conversation. Never forced. But naturally occurring. Now, you may be fatigued at the end of the hour, but you're not fatigued after the first 10 minutes.

And so, I don't think you over get over the fatigue. I think that you build the muscles so that the fatigue hits later and later and later. And one day, you realized, "I can run a seven-minute mile or a four-minute mile or whatever, so let me not try to run a three-minute mile anymore. I'll stop here. I'm good." Each of us will find a place to stop.

As I think about diversity fatigue, some people will come alive with the discussion and they are energized. They are not fatigued by it. They are empowered and enriched and recognized and affirmed by it. And some people just are like, "Look, I'm tired of the issue." There will always be a mix. For younger generations, this topic is tiring already and will eventually retire and die off. Because they live it.

Overall, I don't think you avoid the fatigue. You build the muscle.

Rubén King-Shaw *joined Steward Health Care System in June of 2018 as Chief Strategy Officer. He was named President of Steward Health Care Network (SHCN) in October of that year. SHCN manages* *risk-bearing Accountable Care Organizations in nine states, operates Medicaid and D-SNP MCO in Utah and has a population health MSO. The company deploys tech-enabled services that support high-quality clinical outcomes and optimize total medical expense. Over the course of 2019, Rubén led a team of operators, clinicians, attorneys, technologists and finance executives through a twelve-month process to turnaround Steward's Arizona health plan (Steward Health Choice Arizona) culminating in its sale to Blue Cross Blue Shield of Arizona at a record high valuation. Rubén returned to his role of Chief Strategy Officer in February of 2020 and currently is focused on Stewards expansion into Latin America as well as growth and innovation in the Medicare, Medicaid, and commercial payer markets. Prior to joining the executive management team, Rubén had served as a member of Steward Health Care System's board of directors since its inception in 2010. Rubén is the former Lead Director at Athenahealth and served on the board of directors including Cotiviti Holdings and WellCare Health Plans.*

Throughout his career, Rubén has spent considerable time in public service leading both state and federal government health care benefit programs. Under Florida Governor Jeb Bush, Mr. King-Shaw was the Secretary of the Florida Agency for Health Care Administration. He then served as Deputy Administrator and Chief Operating Officer of the Centers for Medicare and Medicaid Services from 2001 to 2003 during the administration of President George W. Bush. He was also senior advisor to the Secretary of the U.S. Treasury, where he led the Administration's Health Coverage Tax Credit policies to finance coverage for the uninsured. In 2011, Mr. King-Shaw was appointed to the Obama Administration's Program Advisory and Oversight Committee to monitor and provide guidance to Medicare's value-based purchasing program.

Mr. King-Shaw is a Trustee Emeritus of Cornell University and a member of the Board of Overseers for Weil Cornell Medicine. Rubén was also a member of the Board of Trustees of Meharry Medical College in Nashville, TN. Rubén was awarded his B.S. from Cornell University's School of Industrial and Labor Relations in 1983. He earned his Master of International Business at Chapman Graduate School of Business at Florida International University in Miami, Florida and Madrid, Spain. He holds a Masters in Health Services Administration also from Florida International University and in 2007 he completed the postgraduate program in corporate governance at the Harvard Business School.

A True Diversity Conversation With
Juan Mejia, M.P.H.
Senior Vice President & Chief Operating Officer of
New York Presbyterian Lower Manhattan Hospital

TRUE DIVERSITY: Please tell us about your hometown, education, occupation, current role, and any other identifiers that you think are relevant to who you are.

JUAN: I was born and raised in Los Angeles, California. My family is from a small pueblo close to Guadalajara in Mexico. I'm a first generation Mexican-American. Both of my parents were born in Mexico. I lived in LA until the age of 23. This summer will be my 19th year living in NYC... Time flies. So, I guess you can say I'm a New Yorker now!?

However, I am from Los Angeles and that's where I completed most of my education. I went to elementary school and high school in LA and college at UCLA. Shortly after graduating from undergrad, I wanted to pursue my master's degree. Also wanted to leave my home base to have a different perspective on life, so I decided to leave LA and moved to the Big Apple to go to Columbia University to pursue my master's in public health.

My goal was to be in New York City for two years to get my master's and then get back to my home base in LA. While I was here, I fell in love with New York City. I accepted a job at New York Presbyterian Hospital shortly after grad school. I've actually been at New York Presbyterian Hospital ("NYP") for about 17 years. I started my career at NYP as an operations analyst after grad school.

I was an analyst for a couple of years and then transitioned to numerous roles throughout NYP. Today I'm the senior vice president and chief operating officer of one of our hospital campuses, the New York Presbyterian Lower Manhattan Hospital located in Manhattan close to the Brooklyn Bridge. As COO of this hospital, it is my job to run the daily operations of the hospital alongside an amazing team.

Regarding my identifiers, as I mentioned before, my background is of Latino descent and I was raised speaking Spanish and English. Truth be told, while growing up, we spoke more Spanish than English at home.

I identify as a male. I also proudly identify as a gay man. The LGBTQ+ community is a big part of my identity. There are many identifiers that define me, probably a lot more than I've mentioned, but at a high level, that's a little bit of whom I am.

TRUE DIVERSITY: Tell us about being a first generation Mexican-American and the intersection of the two cultures and the impact it has had on you professionally and personally.

JUAN: I was raised in a predominately Mexican neighborhood in LA. So, I grew up with a different perspective of what people normally think of as 'traditional American,' which I learned to appreciate as I got older. The true Latino perspective of America.

When I started middle school, and through high school, I was bussed out of my neighborhood to a predominately white neighborhood. My classmates were somewhat diverse, but interestingly, most of the students of color were bused in from different neighborhoods in LA. My lens of being an American changed as I was now surrounded by friends of different backgrounds. Very different from my neighborhood.

It was interesting... When I first started middle school, many of my classmates said I spoke with an accent. That was news to me.

I was born and raised in this country and never realized I had an accent, and it was strange for me to hear classmates say I did. Reality is... I didn't have an accent; I just spoke differently from friends that came from different neighborhoods.

It was the first time I was reminded that I was a little different from the optics of what people were used to seeing at that school. It was also evident when I went to UCLA. That's probably when I had the biggest growth, and I had to really grow into this bigger and diverse community than my neighborhood and even my high school.

For years, I didn't feel comfortable being a part of that bigger community that looked different than me, and I struggled a bit to find a place where I belonged. I would say that finding a place of belonging is where I had the most growth, especially as I had to learn to adjust to the diversity of the UCLA campus and find my space within it. Even though I was still in Los Angeles, it was a different experience from home.

TRUE DIVERSITY: Tell me about the difference between experiencing being Latino in Los Angeles and New York.

JUAN: There are many similarities but also differences in being a Latino in LA vs NY.

When we think about pie charts that describe us, there are very specific black and white boxes that we all would check off. For me, it would be Latino. I could check off first generation American. I could definitely check off being a gay man, but these boxes alone don't define who I am because I feel like the lens that I live through is not solely reflected by those check boxes, but also the life experience that I've had. It has to do with my upbringing; growing up with my grandmother in a single home where we only spoke Spanish and as a first-generation Mexican-American.

Now add to that my personal experience of merging into the culture in my journey through higher education. Accepting and finding pride in my sexual orientation also formed who I am. Navigating through those experiences in my formative years further shaped my worldview.

Then in my early 20s, I moved to New York to attend Columbia University. While attending Columbia, and for a total of 10 years, I lived in Washington Heights, which is a predominantly Dominican neighborhood in New York City. I quickly learned the similarities and differences in being Dominican vs Mexican Latino. Let's say I learned to appreciate bachata music since moving to NYC.

When you think of my entire life experience, if you follow just those three or four (maybe five) data points that have had a significant impact on me, you realize that can never be captured in a pie chart. Therefore, if I just check off Latino, that won't define me or adequately represent the totality of my experiences. If I just check off that my sexual orientation is gay, and these pie charts are probably similar identifiers to individuals that I grew up with in my family. We're all Latino. I grew up Catholic. We're all first generation. All my cousins are first generation Americans.

We all have very different experiences based on the life that we're living. Some of it has to do with education. Some of it has to do with family. A lot of my cousins have kids. I don't. So, our perspective on life is firmly based on experiences much more than what the pie charts reflect. But it's really the individual life that we experience, and I mentioned before that I run a hospital here.

TRUE DIVERSITY: How have your diverse experiences improved the way you related to your staff and/or patients (consumers)?

JUAN: I find it easy to relate with just about anyone. The first thing that comes to mind is never make assumptions. I was a vice president of a hospital at Washington Heights for many years and the worst thing someone can say is "you know, our patient is Spanish-speaking Latino," and then without knowing the patient make an assumption of what the patient wants or their desires or how they want to receive care. Making assumptions based on the perceived background of the patient without ever having a discussion with the individual can lead to problematic outcomes.

When I talk to person A versus person B, they both might be of the same ethnic or religious backgrounds, but their perspective might be slightly different. Not making assumptions based on a person's perceived identity is one of the most important lessons I've learned in life.

Today, I run a hospital that's in Lower Manhattan which happens to be very close to Chinatown. Naturally, a significant number of our patients are Asian, and the same concepts apply. Although I may not be an expert in Asian culture, it is important that our team is comprised of individuals that are part of, and understand, our local community. My role as a leader is to ensure that we're supporting our teams to think about how to approach our patients, as individual patients, without making assumptions.

TRUE DIVERSITY: You mentioned that you travel a great deal. Tell us how that has affected your perspective and how you approach your job.

JUAN: Yes, I do travel a lot. Love to travel. My favorite part of traveling is getting to know locals from whichever city I'm in and understanding their way of living and what is important to them. It's always interesting for me to see how people perceive Latinos in different countries around the world. It's a reminder of how the world is comprised of many different ways of living, different ideas and thoughts.

Religion plays an important factor within some countries that I visit. It plays a lot less of a factor in other countries. Sexuality is openly talked about in many countries that I visit, and it's not in other countries that I visited. The variances really allow me to understand and fully appreciate differences in culture.

It allows me to appreciate diverse thought as opposed to me trying to impose the American way of being or thinking. Because when I go abroad, it's actually the opposite.

TRUE DIVERSITY: How do you encourage cultural inclusion or empower people to show up with all of this contextual cultural information?

JUAN: In the workplace, it comes down to ensuring that all voices are included across our teams. In a hospital, this could mean having staff councils to ensure that staff across all our departments have a voice on hospital initiatives. Generally speaking, our frontline teams at the hospital are diverse. If we create that space for staff to share their diverse opinions, then management can appropriately respond to any issues that arise from the lens of the diversity of our frontline staff, which reflects the diversity of our patients.

The higher you go up in leadership levels across most large organizations, you will notice less diversity at the top. When you get to the C-suite (high-ranking executives), as an example, it's far less diverse. This is true across the nation and the reality of most hospitals across the country. There's a huge shortage of people of color in the C-suite.

As we think of diversity in leadership the question then becomes, "What do we do differently from a recruiting perspective to promote diversity at that level?"

At the C-suite level, we often have recruiting firms to help provide us with qualified candidates for specific jobs. The question I would ask is, "Are we pushing our recruiters to provide a diverse pool of qualified candidates to the table?"

Far too often there is no diversity within a very large pool of candidates for executive-level jobs at hospitals. Do we have enough women, people of color, LGBTQ, and other qualified candidates in the pool? If there's no diversity in the candidate pool, then you can't shift the paradigm of that C-Suite. Therefore, it is imperative for all of us at executive levels to push from within the organization not only to have diversity on the frontlines, but throughout the organization and at the highest executive levels.

I am on the board of a health professional organizations and we often have discussions about Latino executive representation across the country. A valid question that often comes up is, "What are we doing to promote a diverse pipeline of young individuals who will be our future directors, vice presidents or senior vice presidents at hospitals in the next five to ten years and beyond?"

Part of the key to success is developing mentoring programs and working with students at the undergraduate and graduate levels. Working on that pipeline is very important to ensure that the demographics at executive levels change, which will lead to a positive change with diversity in thought across our organizations.

I can say that diversity and inclusion is an important part of the fabric at New York Presbyterian Hospital. One of the things that I take pride in is leading our LGBTQ+ strategy group which is responsible for setting policies, training, community programs, and many other things for our patients and employees. Having teams that lead important initiatives to represent our diverse communities is critical across all organizations and in society as a whole.

As leaders, it's our responsibility to be sure that our staff's diverse perspectives are represented at the table.

TRUE DIVERSITY: Do you think that is happening because you're a member of the broader LGBT table and at the decision-making table? Or, do you think it would happen without you being there?

JUAN: I'm fortunate to be part of an organization that truly values diversity and inclusion. But that's not the reality of all organizations around us. As leaders, we have the ability to drive change in our organizations. I used the LGBTQ+ strategy group that we have at NYP as an example because I'm very passionate about it. Not just because I identify as a gay man, but because this continues to be an area where healthcare organizations need to focus to ensure that we are providing equitable care to all patients.

TRUE DIVERSITY: Having diverse representation at the highest levels is very important in terms of making diversity a real thing for any organization.

JUAN: Yes. I've discussed this very topic at different leadership forums. There are a lot of individuals doing grassroot efforts at hospitals or medical schools across the country to try to drive change—which is great. The first thing I tell everyone is to find an ally on the senior leadership team that supports the diversity agenda. Once you have buy-in at the senior leadership team level, then the rest of the work is doable.

Without buy-in in the senior leadership group, it's harder to drive change. Not impossible, just harder. So, I always tell everyone to leverage resources to find that individual who is going to push the same agenda for you at the senior management level at your organization.

TRUE DIVERSITY: Is there a hierarchy in your identifiers that you think are more directly related to who you are or is it a hodgepodge?

JUAN: No, it's definitely a hodgepodge. There's definitely no hierarchy... I see myself through a lens of varying life experiences. It all depends on the circumstances and my surroundings, but there's definitely no pecking order amongst Mexican-American, gay, male, etc. Life experiences define who I am as opposed to the three or four, maybe five checkboxes that I could potentially check off.

TRUE DIVERSITY: What does diversity mean to you?

JUAN: Diversity is representation of individuals with distinct backgrounds, including individuals of different ethnicity, gender, sexual orientation, socioeconomic status, and life experiences. Diversity is about having a diverse pool of individuals with a diverse pool of thought.

As an organization, when you have a diverse pool of thought, you make the best decisions. At our NYP, diversity in thought positively impacts our 50,000+ employees and our hundreds of thousands of patients that come through our doors every single day.

So, it's really that diverse thought that enables organizations to excel in performance.

TRUE DIVERSITY: How do we avoid so-called diversity fatigue?

JUAN: When people start thinking about diversity as defined quotas, we lose the underlying essence of diversity. It's not about meeting the minimum number of people… It's about discussing *why* diversity is important. Why is it important to have different backgrounds?

When you focus on the why we're doing something versus hitting certain quotas, then you won't have so much fatigue. The focus should be on understanding why it is important that we have diverse teams or diversity across the board; whether it's in education or diversity amongst our teams and different organizations. If we focus more on the *why* as opposed to the numbers, it helps to avoid fatigue. Let's be clear, these issues are never going away. Our country and our world are becoming more diverse as time progresses, so it's a discussion that we cannot—and should not—avoid.

We all benefit as communities by ensuring that we have diversity and ensuring that we have equal representation across teams. This is very important in healthcare. But even in our local community, if we have community boards or anything else.

TRUE DIVERSITY: Is there anything else you would like to add?

JUAN: The concept of seeing people through pie charts is problematic. Understanding the people and communities around us is most important. We understand people by understanding the lens through which they see life. Appreciating our differences makes us a better community. How boring would it be if we were all the same!

Juan Mejia, M.P.H., *is Senior Vice President & Chief Operating Officer of New York-Presbyterian Lower Manhattan Hospital. In this role, he manages day-to-day operations, oversees operating and capital budgets, and implements clinical strategy. Since joining New York-Presbyterian in 2003, Mr. Mejia has served in several roles including Revenue Manager and Director of Clinical Operations at NYP Milstein, Director of the Gastrointestinal Service Line at NYP/Columbia, and Vice President of Operations at NYP Morgan Stanley Children's Hospital. Most recently, he served as Vice President, Operations for NYP/Weill Cornell Hospital. Prior to joining New York-Presbyterian, he was a consultant for the New York City Department of Health and Mental Hygiene where he worked closely with community-based organizations to reduce infant mortality. Mr. Mejia earned his Master of Public Health from the Mailman School of Public Health at Columbia University and his Bachelor's in Physiological Science from the University of California Los Angeles.*

A True Diversity Conversation With
Shideh Sedgh Bina
Founding Partner, Insigniam

TRUE DIVERSITY: Please tell us your hometown, education, occupation, current role, and any other identifiers that you think are relevant to who you are.

SHIDEH: I'm almost 60 years old. I will be 60 in a couple of months. I emigrated from Iran in 1963 with my family. I was 3.5 years old. We were a non-Muslim minority. I grew up in New York and then I came to Philadelphia to go to school and I started an international management consulting firm over 30 years ago. We have offices in Europe, outside of Philadelphia, and outside of Los Angeles, and I work with very large multinational organizations on how to generate breakthrough performance, innovation, or transformation.

TRUE DIVERSITY: Tell us about immigrating to the United States, growing up in New York and Philadelphia, being an immigrant, and whether that had any impact on you.

SHIDEH: Being an immigrant in 1963 from this 'weird' country called Iran that no one ever heard of was a pretty big deal, and so I would say one of the most formative experiences that I had to overcome for most of my life, which I actually later probably parlayed into a big lever for my success, is that I was considered an outsider.

Part of what I do is culture work with organizations that want to transform organizational culture. I understand culture from the deep profound fact of having experienced it. I used to not understand how people knew certain rules and certain ways. I remember asking the same question to my friends after I would make some kind of faux pas or just not get what was going with a cultural norm that I was experiencing at the time. I would ask, "Do you have some book you read or something? How do you know these things that I just don't know?"

When I was in college, I read a book called "The Silent Language" by Edward Hall where he really distinguishes culture. In his case it's social cultures, and I then understood that there was a silent language that I was not aware of that spoke to what it meant to be an American. And also, inside of that, the expected role of women in the American culture is very different than in the Iranian culture.

My family did everything to blend into the culture. We ate New York foods, tried various activities, yet still I didn't quite get the rhythm—I was one beat off. I mean, I ended up being pretty popular in high school, but I had to do this stuff you have to do. I still felt out of place, and then I got accepted to an Ivy League school, The University of Pennsylvania. The funny thing is I didn't even know it was an Ivy League school. I just knew that I loved the school when I visited it with my aunt who lived in Philadelphia, and then by the time I got to college, it was during a hostage situation in Iran.

So, I had hidden my name. I had gone by the name Sheila most of my life because people made fun of the name Shideh, which turned into 'Shideet,' which turned into 'shithead' quickly. So, I had become Sheila, but I decided in college that I was going to stop the camouflage of myself.

Prior to the hostage situation in Iran, I was able to do business with Iran because I'm fluent in Farsi. In 1977, it quickly changed from a good thing to something that was not considered favorable.

TRUE DIVERSITY: How has being of Iranian descent changed for your over the years?

SHIDEH: I think you're going to find a theme that I was an outsider, right? I went to Wharton when I was 17 years old. I was younger than everyone because I'd skipped a grade before college and then, when I went to the business school in 1977, only ten to fifteen percent of the students were women.

So that theme, right? I'm just different. Then I started my business when I was 30, and I'm younger than most other business owners, particularly in my field. I had a male partner, and at one point, he used to do a lot of the heavy sales pitches and presentations. He had a sales background, and then one day we had a really big pitch, and he couldn't come. I was going to go by myself.

I'll never forget it. I believe it was 1991, and we were pitching to a chemical company. I walked into a boardroom of twelve men in suits that looked alike, and I remember being terrified, and my partner said to me, "We're either going to become this culture or we're going to intervene in that culture." That really has been my stance. It's all about just unprecedented intentional discontinuity. That's why it started to become something I could use because I could think differently.

Then, we developed methods to support people to provoke them to think differently, and so now, not going with the flow is probably one of my strengths. I am very palatable to the flow. I married an Iranian man even though neither of us intended to marry an Iranian, but we did. I also think about my sons and the fact that they were able to participate in sports. Title IX came out when I was in high school, so a woman in sports was not common then. I use sports as an example; however, all of those things—the differences between the way men and women are socialized in culture—have an impact.

The only thing I remember is a Girl Scouts badge. You know, we used to have little teams that got badges in Girl Scouts. I went on one Girl Scout camping trip with a few mothers. That's a big piece that's silent, but so prevalent in shaping you.

Can you imagine walking into business school and then a work environment as a woman back then? It's different now, and I definitely see with the girls my sons associated with that their experiences were different. Finally, a different, equal mindset. Nowadays, I don't hear the girls holding back their ambition or their choices because of the men they're with or society. It's a completely different worldview for women than when I was growing up in America.

TRUE DIVERSITY: Do you think there is a disconnect between the women of your generation and women of later generations?

SHIDEH: I wouldn't call it a disconnect. I think it's an evolution. I think it's a welcomed evolution that the younger women had come to expect a world with an even playing field.

Now, how that plays out in their careers, I don't see it. But I do see that they love being around me, younger women. There's still a scarcity of women role models. I remember having to write a college essay when I was applying for college and it was like one of the questions was, "If you could pick anyone from history that you could have dinner with, who would you pick?"

I couldn't find women. I couldn't think of women in history. I mean there were some exceptions. Queen Elizabeth I, Queen Victoria. But if you ever read her story, she had to deal with a lot with her husband.

Not having female role models was a real crisis for me. Today, there are far more women who are in leadership roles that can be modeled. In fact, I had the opportunity to meet Hillary Clinton at one point, and I spoke to her about how excited I was that there was somebody for young girls to look up to in the public arena.

That is the silent language. Those are things that shape your expectations of the world.

TRUE DIVERSITY: What does the word diversity mean to you?

SHIDEH: To me, diversity means enough difference that sameness is not expected.

TRUE DIVERSITY: Can you expand on that in the context of our TRUE DIVERSITY discussion?

SHIDEH: To be clear, I'm not a diversity consultant. I'm a management breakthrough results consultant. However, it is still just teaching people to be able to deal with diverse styles and thinking. He thinks from a quantitative framework or she thinks from a quantitative framework. This person thinks from a big picture frame. That person likes to mull over things. That person needs to speak out loud to figure things out. Just that basic level. What's the opposite of homogeneous?

TRUE DIVERSITY: Heterogeneous.

SHIDEH: Yes, heterogeneous. Thank you. I'm talking about real basic diversity now. I always say to people, you need to learn to speak different languages. If I'm sitting with someone who has a quantitative frame through which they look at life or business, I have to speak to them in that language. So, diversity would express itself as I'm going to get over to your world and talk in a context that is relevant to where you're living.

TRUE DIVERSITY: How do you communicate the power of diversity of thought and its complement to innovation and driving results to your clients?

SHIDEH: Well, I had this real insight recently that was very interesting. A client had said this to me years ago, and I didn't quite get it. He said, "Now I'm talking about psychometric profiles." Using the big five-personality model, or there's the Jungian psychology, which is less empirically validated.

Introvert or extrovert. Big picture sensory. He said to me once, "Shideh, you know, diverse teams are sometimes more difficult." I thought, "What is he talking about?" I didn't understand what he meant until years later, after I had done a lot of consulting with leadership and executive groups. They clump in the same area of psychometric profiles. I've come to see that it's easier to get along with people who think like you. When you get a real diverse team where there are people who are people-focused and other people who are quantitative-focused and other people who are qualitative focused, it's difficult because you have to manage the diverse thinking. But we're not taught how to navigate differences. So, I think we keep looking for sameness rather than looking for differentness primarily because it's easier to navigate.

TRUE DIVERSITY: But does it really push the conversation forward if there are no other perspectives?

SHIDEH: Oftentimes I will go into teams and there's a couple of outliers and they're often discounted. Remember, the word nonsense is no sense. It comes from no sense, which is the opposite of common sense. People who don't fit the common sense are considered to have no sense and are often discounted because they are outliers.

How do you work on that and change that within the team? I will give you an example from my company. Recently, we hired an incredibly talented woman. First of all, I started this firm with two men and a woman, and we are majority-owned by women, which is a great achievement. Our partners are equity partners. They get to be partners by merit. It's a complete meritocracy, and the majority of our partners now are women.

The company just received an award from the Healthcare Business Women's Association for the equity in our firm leadership, and we happen to be different than our peer companies. But, you know, not different enough, right?

As I mentioned, we hired a younger woman who is new to consulting. She wasn't someone who was in the business for 20 years. She's approximately four years out of college who was raised in the Caribbean and did not come from a corporate background, although she has an incredible education, a solid CV, and more importantly, the grit to accomplish great things.

I love it because I'm challenged as a leader on how to draw the best out of her. How do I coach her to be able to allow people to connect with her, but not lose her differentness? Because she's different than what you're going to find in the corporate world. It's a real challenge because you can easily squash someone like that.

TRUE DIVERSITY: How did you develop that management skill? What caused you to do so?

SHIDEH: I don't think you can do the work we do for 30 years on project after project, huge initiatives, transformation after transformation, and not develop an aptitude for managing difference.

I have seen the laws of the universe reversed, so to speak. Someone says, "This can't be done." Then a year later, it's done. You can't do that for 30 years without understanding that nothing is fixed in stone.

I had to develop a certain mental agility to be a professional breakthrough thinker and transformationalist. I want it to be a business transformation, not airy-fairy land, which is what the stereotype is. Having that kind of mental agility is just part of our craft in the work that we do.

I've sat at the tables of almost any discussion from supply chain strategy to talent, you know, but after 30 years, we've seen and danced enough to know, because we're consultants; we are not industry-agnostic. We're in all industries. You just get that you need to have and understand the rainbow.

TRUE DIVERSITY: How do we overcome so-called diversity fatigue? How do we drive home the thought that diversity is not some pie-in-the-sky PC thing, but it really is about driving the bottom line?

SHIDEH: Well, I do have a particular sensitive spot for gender diversity, so I'm always looking there first. I mean, there's a whole lot of statistics out there about how it's good for performance.

Catalyst, which is a women's workplace advocacy think tank, published a report that showed that performance is better in organizations that have gender parity or close to gender parity.

I don't think the issue is will at this point. Collectively I think there is enough will because it's just the way the gravity is moving. I think that people don't know what they don't know about how they think.

I think people have blind spots, so I would work more on people getting cognizant of how they see and therefore how their logic and process that leads to a lack of diversity. For example, when someone dresses different than you, how do you discount him or her? You know, what do you do? It's back to that silent language that people don't know what they don't know. Maybe I'm being a Pollyanna, but I don't think the percentage of people who were against creating diversity is low enough for that not to be the reason.

I truly believe the great majority of people just don't know. So, I said they don't know what they don't know about what they're doing. If you asked someone, "Did you notice that you check to see whether your door is locked moving through a neighborhood where there're more people of color?" They don't even know that they're doing that.

TRUE DIVERSITY: True, most people are unaware of their unconscious biases. Hence, why it's unconscious.

SHIDEH: Yes, and I would be careful of using terms that people disconnect from immediately, like unconscious bias. Unconscious bias has now become one of those words that people don't think about any more when they hear that word. So, I think we have to keep finding ways to pierce the hypnosis. I was just thinking of my husband as a feminist. I can't even tell you how much of a feminist he is, if there's such a thing for a man to be a feminist. My husband has never in any way expected me to be any different or to hold myself back or some kind of shrinking violet personality.

We've even raised our sons, we hope, to be multidimensional thinkers, their feelings, their thoughts, their brawn, all of that.

TRUE DIVERSITY: Like you said, people usually hear the word "bias" and they turn off their brains. We call it blind spots.

SHIDEH: We all must find different terminology so people don't stop thinking when they hear these trigger words. In my conversation with you, I started calling it the silent language. I don't always call it that. But the most important thing I think is what we say is if you want to have breakthrough thinking, you've got to reveal what's already there and unhook it to create new thinking.

You can't just put new thinking without knowing and being aware of what your old thinking is.

Shideh Sedgh Bina *is a founding partner of Insigniam and the Editor-In-Chief of IQ Insigniam Quarterly®. She is responsible for the firm's business development and marketing, Shideh has over thirty years of experience in management and consulting. She possesses expertise in working with CEOs and other C-Suite executives to generate and execute enterprise-wide transformation in an array of industries, such as health care delivery, life-sciences, retail, media, and fast-moving consumer goods.*

PharmaVOICE named Shideh one of the 100 Most Inspiring People in Life-Sciences in 2016, and in 2014 the Healthcare Businesswomen's Association named her Woman of the Year. She has been a speaker at numerous executive conferences for Fortune 500 companies and she was an adjunct faculty member at St. Joseph's University's Haub School of Business. She has authored dozens of articles and her work has been featured in Fortune and Reuters.

Shideh is a Trustee of the Committee for Economic Development—a nonprofit, nonpartisan, business-led, public policy organization—and a member of the National Association of Corporate Directors.

In 1990, Shideh co-founded High Performance Consulting, which merged with the Rosenberg Group in 2005 to create Insigniam. Prior to her work in management consulting, Shideh conceived, owned, and managed a profitable upscale retail business before selling it to her employees. She then led and managed the New England region for an international training and development firm.

She holds a B.S. in Economics from The Wharton School at the University of Pennsylvania.

Acknowledgments

I would like to start by thanking my wife, Jennifer. From the very first thought of a book to the final manuscript, she was an encouraging voice keeping me focused on the completion of the book. Thank you, Jen.

Thank you to my 3 beautiful daughters Desiree, Lauren and Sarah who embody the messages in the book. All three are advocates for women and minority issues. To Desiree for ensuring that my sometimes-direct messages would land on accepting ears. To Lauren for helping me develop the mathematical concepts associated with the Diversity Quotient. To Sarah for helping me see the bigger picture and talk through the concepts in the book. You represent true inspiration to me and everyone you come in contact with.

To my mom and dad, Rosa and Nilo, for being an inspiration to any immigrant that comes to America. They inspired me to write this book through their actions, not words. My mom masterminded the exodus from Cuba and has always been a driver for personal achievement. My dad passed away last year. He remains the most unselfish man that I have ever known. His eagerness to help others motivated my writing.

To my brother and sister, Luis and Lourdes, for not making me feel too much like a middle child as I grew up. They are a great example of True Diversity because although both Hispanics, they extremely diverse in thought, insight gathering and contributions.

Thank you to Nathan Williams, my co-author. Nathan is an incredible inspiration - to me as a first-time author but more importantly, for living the premises found within True Diversity and championing the cause of minorities nationwide.

Thank you to Sherice Torres for investing her time to read TRUE DIVERSITY and for sharing her story and insights in an appropriate and perfectly written FOREWARD.

I would like to thank Marion Brooks. Marion is a leader in Corporate Diversity and a best-selling author of "What You Don't Know Is Hurting You". The completion of his book and the impact it is having on younger minorities has been an incredible inspiration.

To Bruce Epstein, Founder of RevHealth, an advertising firm that welcomes, develops and promotes minorities and women in an otherwise male dominated industry. Walking the walk speaks louder than any book.

I would like to thank all the "kids" that influenced me at Memorial Park, the greatest turf to learn about diversity. A special thank you to Jose Ortea, Sergio Garabito, Carlos Rodriguez and Jorge Hernandez for keeping in touch and keeping the memories of Memorial Park alive.

To the entire Pegasys Team at Roche, especially Brian Murphy, George Harb, Luis Mendez, Juan Carlos Lopez-Talavera, Chris Pappas, Mike Tunkelrott, Gary Choy, Devrim Aran, Omar Ahmed, Dane Hartung, Frank Griffith, Jessie Tombalakian, Jen Campagna, Rene Bobal, George Gauthier, Frank Griffith, James Brooks and Harry Dunston, most diverse team to ever launch a Pharmaceutical product in the US. This team demonstrated the incredible power of a diverse team. The greatest Harvard Business Review case never written!

I have worked for many bosses over 37 years in the Pharmaceutical Industry. A few stand out as natural leaders that understand the power of True Diversity. Alex Gorsky for genuinely caring about and leading from the top. Alex continues to be an inspiration to thousands at J&J, worldwide. Larry Somerville for providing advise and mentoring in the early stages of my career. To Jerry Acuff, the greatest sales coach that I have ever met and the person who encourage me to write a book. To Frank Condella for seeing what others could not see when he took a chance on me and leading the push towards diversity on the Pegasys Team. A special thank you to Georges Gemayel, a great friend, mentor and inspiration. Georges is the only boss that I can think of that would have allowed me to assemble the Pegasys Team (you must look at the chart in the book) where diversity, intellect, tenacity and individual competence out-weighed industry tenure.

A different kind of thank you to my most recent boss, Kyle Ferguson. After being "restructured" out of my previous role, it took me 21 months to land a job. Kyle took a chance on a 59-year-old, minority candidate - something that most people would not do. Trust me, I applied for over 100 roles on LinkedIn and Indeed and received zero interview offers - just letters stating that I was "overqualified". "Overqualified" is the euphemism for "too old" and the legal way of discriminating by age. Believe me when I say this, "the greatest discriminating factor in the American workforce today isn't race, color, sex etc. - it is age. Don't get me wrong, of course there are inequities faced by minorities but when you add age to the mix you get an older aged minority - now, try getting the job you want with those two compounding factors."

Thank you to our editor Keith Gordon for ensuring that our message flows to our readers.

Thank you to Shideh Sedgwick Bina, Juan Mejia, Ruben King-Shaw, Fleur Lee and Antonius Porch for sharing your stories, experiences and insights that make True Diversity come to life because you have been living the writings in the book. The interviews represent the most critical concept of True Diversity - that amongst 5 distinguished minorities, you are extremely diverse! Thank you for taking the time to be interviewed by Nathan and for providing an impressive dose of realism to True Diversity.

Thank you to thank the following organizations that contributed by providing examples of how we can work in a True Diversity manner: Hoffman-LaRoche, Forbes, UNC Chapel Hill, North Carolina State University, Harvard University, Maritz, MIT, Johnson & Johnson, Delta Point, Marriott, Publix, McKinsey & Co, Deloitte Consulting, Catalyst Learning, Accenture, Mastercard, Bank of America, Qantas Airlines, Gallup Organization, Walmart, Apple, Boston Consulting Group, Diversity Inc, The Diversity Officer Magazine, Coca-Cola, SHRM.

My last thank you is to those who have confided in me and allowed me to mentor you. What you don't realize is that you were also mentoring me because I learned so much from each of you, thank you for your teachings! I am so proud of you- Cintia Piccina, Steven Jackson, Doug Yurubi, Ruth Clements, Jeff Baynes, Emile Williams, Carolyn Berg, Harmonie Franklin, Liz Taylor-Farr, Luis Perez, Jorge Luna, Catherine Ross, Michael Nesrallah, Andrea Shultz, Leverne Marsh, Uneek Mehra, Lane Wilson, Kevin Clark, Sundip Raval, Rahul Bhatia and Drayton Wise.

Thank you and God Bless America for the opportunities that you have given my family and minorities from all over the world.

Bibliography

Apple Inc. "Open." Accessed October 3, 2017.

Babcock, Pamela. "5 Steps to Improve Diversity Recruiting." SHRM. February 24, 2017. https://www.shrm.org/resourcesandtools/hr-topics/talent-acquisition/pages/five-steps-improve-diversity-recruiting.aspx.

Blank, Charlotte. "5 Ways to Tackle Bias in the Workplace." TLNT. July 20, 2018. https://www.tlnt.com/5-was-to-tackle-bias-in-the-workplace/.

Bourke, Juliet, and Bernadette Dillon. "The Diversity and Inclusion Revolution: Eight Powerful Truths." *Deloitte Review*, no. 22 (January 2018): 82-95. https://www2.deloitte.com/us/en/insights/deloitte-review/issue-22/diversity-and-inclusion-at-work-eight-powerful-truths.html.

Business Dictionary. "Cultural Intelligence (CQ)." Accessed August 23, 2020. http://www.businessdictionary.com/definition/cultural-intelligence-CQ.html.

Business for Trans Equality. "Home." Accessed August 24, 2020, https://businessfortransequality.com/.

Camerer, Colin, George Loewenstein, and Martin Weber. "The Curse of Knowledge in Economic Settings: An Experimental Analysis." PDF file. *Journal of Political Economy* 97, no. 5 (1989): 1232-1254. https://www.cmu.edu/dietrich/sds/docs/loewenstein/CurseknowledgeEconSet.pdf.

CareerCast Diversity. "How to identify Hidden biases." Accessed August 23, 2020. https://diversity.careercast.com/article/how-identify-hidden-biases.

Catalyst. "Diversity Fatigue in the Workplace: How to Get Unstuck." August 7, 2019. https://www.catalyst.org/2019/08/07/diversity-fatigue/.

Chhun, Bunkhuon. "Better Decisions Through Diversity." Kellogg Insights. October 1, 2010. https://insight.kellogg.northwestern.edu/article/better_decisions_through_diversity.

Comaford, Christine. "How to Work with Unconscious Bias in your Organization." Forbes. June 25, 2016. https://www.forbes.com/sites/christinecomaford/2016/06/25/how-leaders-bust-unconscious-biases-in-business/#4e8e4d862c66.

Cultural Intelligence Center. "About." Accessed August 23, 2020. https://culturalq.com/about-cultural-intelligence/.

DiversityInc. "About the DiversityInc. top 50 Process." Accessed August 24, 2020. https://www.diversityinc.com/about-the-diversityinc-top-50-process/.

DiversityInc. "Accenture." Accessed August 24, 2020. https://www.diversityinc.com/accenture/.

DiversityInc. "Hall of Fame | Johnson & Johnson." Accessed August 24, 2020. https://www.diversityinc.com/johnson-johnson-hall-of-fame/.

DiversityInc. "Marriott International." Accessed August 24, 2020. https://www.diversityinc.com/marriott-international/.

Dobbin, Frank, Alexandra Kalev, and Erin Kelly. "Diversity management in Corporate America." PDF File. *Contexts* 6, no. 4 (Fall 2007): 21-27. https://scholar.harvard.edu/dobbin/files/2007_contexts_dobbin_kalev_kelly.pdf.

Earley, P. Christopher, and Elaine Mosakowski. "Cultural Intelligence." Harvard Business Review. October 2004. https://hbr.org/2004/10/cultural-intelligence.

Employers for Pay Equity. "Home." Accessed August 24, 2020. http://www.employersforpayequity.com/.

Fan, Donald. "Proof that Diversity Drives Innovation." DiversityInc. August 31, 2011, https://www.diversityinc.com/proof-that-diversity-drives-innovation/.

Gonda, Rob. "Adaptability Is Key to Survival In the Age of Digital Darwinism." Forbes. May 24, 2018. https://www.forbes.com/sites/forbestechcouncil/2018/05/24/adaptability-is-key-to-survival-in-the-age-of-digital-darwinism/#5e094793408c.

Great Place to Work. "Fortune 100 Best Companies to Work For® 2019." Accessed August 24, 2020. https://www.greatplacetowork.com/best-workplaces/100-best/2019.

Hewett, Jackson. "Alan Joyce says management diversity was key to getting Qantas through turbulent times." The Australian. March 4, 2016.

Hsu, Hua. "The Year in 'Diversity Fatigue.'" The New Yorker. December 26, 2017. https://www.newyorker.com/culture/2017-in-review/the-year-in-diversity-fatigue.

Hunt, Vivian, Dennis Layton, and Sara Prince. "Why diversity Matters." McKinsey & Company. January 1, 2015. https://www.mckinsey.com/business-functions/organization/our-insights/why-diversity-matters.

Johansson, Frans. *The Medici Effect: Breakthroughs Insights at the Intersection of Ideas, Concepts, and Cultures.* Cambridge: Harvard Business School Publishing, 2004.

Johnson & Johnson. "Credo." Accessed August 23, 2020. https://www.jnj.com/credo/.

Johnson & Johnson. "Diversity & Inclusion." Accessed August 23, 2020. https://www.jnj.com/about-jnj/diversity.

Kaplan, Mark, and Mason Donovan. *The Inclusion Dividend: Why Investing in Diversity and Inclusion Pays Off.* Boston: Bibliomotion Books & Media, 2013.

Kennedy, Jane. "Debiasing the Curse of Knowledge in Audit Judgment." *The Accounting Review* 70, no. 2 (April 1995): 249-273.

Lindsay, Alex, Eden King, Michelle Hebl, and Noah Levine "The Impact of Method, Motivation, and Empathy on Diversity Training Effectiveness." *Journal of Business Psychology* 30 (2015): 605-617. https://doi.org/10.1007/s10869-014-9384-3.

Livermore, David A. *Driven By Difference: How Great Companies Fuel Innovation Through Diversity.* New York: American Management Association, 2016.

Lorenzo, Rocío, Nicole Voigt, Karin Schetelig, Annika Zawadzki, Isabelle Welpe, and Prisca Brosi. "The Mix That Matters: Innovation Through Diversity." Boston Consulting Group. April 26, 2017, https://www.bcg.com/publications/2017/people-organization-leadership-talent-innovation-through-diversity-mix-that-matters.

Mander, Lloyd. "Relational analytics: Ideation, innovation and diverse thinking." Diversity of thought blog. February 1, 2019. https://diversityofthought.co.nz/blog/f/relational-analytics-ideation-innovation-and-diverse-thinking.

Mastercard. "Diversity and Inclusion." Accessed August 24, 2020. https://www.mastercard.us/en-us/about-mastercard/who-we-are/diversity-inclusion.html.

Merriam-Webster Collegiate Dictionary. 11th ed. Springfield: Merriam-Webster, 2019.

Navarro, Renee. "Unconscious Bias."University of California, San Francisco. Accessed August 23, 2020. https://diversity.ucsf.edu/resources/unconscious-bias.

Nester, Katharine. "Diversity, Innovation and Opportunity: Why You Need A Diverse Product Engineering Team." Forbes. July 31, 2018. https://www.forbes.com/sites/forbestechcouncil/2018/07/31/diversity-innovation-and-opportunity-why-you-need-a-diverse-product-engineering-team/#5d63bd4f3e33.

Office of Management and Budget. "Revisions to the Standards for the Classification of Federal Data on Race and Ethnicity." Obama White House. Accessed August 24, 2020. https://obamawhitehouse.archives.gov/omb/fedreg_1997standards.

Paradigm for Parity. "About." Accessed August 24, 2020. https://www.paradigm4parity.com/about#who-we-are.

Publix. "Publix Makes Fortune's 100 Best Companies to Work For List for 23rd Straight Year." February 18, 2020. https://corporate.publix.com/about-publix/newsroom/news-releases/publix-makes-fortunes-100-best-companies-to-work-for-23-straight-years.

Reeves, Martin, and Mike Deimler. "Adaptability: The New Competitive Advantage." Harvard Business Review. July 2011. https://hbr.org/2011/07/adaptability-the-new-competitive-advantage.

Ruby. "About." Accessed August 23, 2020. https://www.ruby.com/about-ruby/.

Sabel, Jon-Mark. "5 Steps to Reduce Bias in the Workplace." HireVue. April 23, 2018. https://www.hirevue.com/blog/5-steps-to-mitigating-bias-in-the-workplace.

Schiller, Ben. "Want A More Innovative Company? Simple: Hire A More Diverse Workforce." Fast Company. January 12, 2018. https://www.fastcompany.com/40515712/want-a-more-innovative-company-simple-hire-a-more-diverse-workforce.

Shook, Ellyn, and Julie Sweet. "Getting to Equal 2019: Creating a Culture That Drives Innovation." Accenture. Accessed August 24, 2020. https://www.accenture.com/us-en/about/inclusion-diversity/gender-equality-innovation-research.

UNC Gillings School of Global Public Health. "Open-ended responses from student-conducted survey, 28 April 2010." PDF file. July 2013. https://sph.unc.edu/files/2013/07/define_diversity.pdf.

Ungerleider, Neal. "Startup Culture's Lack of Diversity Stifles Innovation." Fast Company, July 18, 2013. https://www.fastcompany.com/3014434/startup-cultures-lack-of-diversity-stifles-innovation.

Vaughn, Billy. "The Top Ten Culturally Competent Interviewing Strategies." Diversity Officer Magazine. Accessed August 24, 2020. https://diversityofficermagazine.com/cultural-competence/the-top-ten-culturally-competent-interviewing-strategies/.

Walker, Tat Bellamy, and Richard Feloni. "Here's the presentation google gives employees on how to spot unconscious bias at work." Business Insider. June 8, 2020. https://www.businessinsider.com/google-unconscious-bias-training-presentation-2015-12.

Yehia, Yasmine. "The Importance of Cultural Intelligence in International Business." Global Edge. February 16, 2018. https://globaledge.msu.edu/blog/post/55562/the-importance-of-cultural-intelligence.

"Race and Ethnic Standards for Federal Statistics and Administrative Reporting. "CDC. Last modified November 19, 2019. https://wonder.cdc.gov/wonder/help/populations/bridged-race/directive15.html.

Endnotes

1 Source: Nickelodeon Universe

2 Source: "The Power Of Belonging: What it Means and Why It Matters in Today's Workplace"

3 Merriam-Webster Collegiate Dictionary, 11th ed. (2019), s.v. "Diversity."

4 Mark Kaplan and Mason Donovan, The Inclusion Dividend: Why Investing in Diversity and Inclusion Pays Off (Boston: Bibliomotion Books & Media, 2013), 9.

5 "Open-ended responses from student-conducted survey, 28 April 2010," UNC Gillings School of Global Public Health, July 2013, https://sph.unc.edu/files/2013/07/define_diversity.pdf.

6 David A. Livermore, Driven By Difference: How Great Companies Fuel Innovation Through Diversity (New York: American Management Association, 2016), 8.

7 Merriam-Webster Collegiate Dictionary, 11th ed. (2019), s.v. "Quotient."

8 "Credo," Johnson & Johnson, accessed August 23, 2020, https://www.jnj.com/credo/.

9 "Diversity & Inclusion," Johnson & Johnson, accessed August 23, 2020, https://www.jnj.com/about-jnj/diversity.

10 Vivian Hunt, Dennis Layton, and Sara Prince, "Why diversity Matters," McKinsey & Company, January 1, 2015, https://www.mckinsey.com/business-functions/organization/our-insights/why-diversity-matters.

11 Hunt, Layton, and Prince.

12 Hunt, Layton, and Prince, "Why Diversity Matters."

13 Hunt, Layton, and Prince.

14 Hunt, Layton, and Prince.

15 Hunt, Layton, and Prince, "Why Diversity Matters."

16 Hunt, Layton, and Prince, "Why Diversity Matters."

17 Juliet Bourke and Bernadette Dillon, "The Diversity and Inclusion Revolution: Eight Powerful Truths," Deloitte Review, no. 22 (January 2018): 82-97.

18 https://www2.deloitte.com/us/en/insights/deloitte-review/issue-22/diversity-and-inclusion-at-work-eight-powerful-truths.html.

19 Bourke and Dillon, 84 .

20 Bourke and Dillon, 84.

21 Bourke and Dillon, "The Diversity and Inclusion Revolution," 84.

22 Kaplan and Donovan, The Inclusion Dividend, 35.

23 Donald Fan, "Proof that Diversity Drives Innovation," DiversityInc, August 31, 2011, https://www.diversityinc.com/proof-that-diversity-drives-innovation/.

24 Jackson Hewett, "Alan Joyce says management diversity was key to getting Qantas through turbulent times," The Australian, March 4, 2016.

25 Bourke and Dillon, "The Diversity and inclusion revolution," 83.

26 Hewett, "Alan Joyce."

27 Bourke and Dillon, "The Diversity and inclusion revolution," 83.

28 "Open," Apple, Inc., accessed October 3, 2017.

29 Colin Camerer, George Loewenstein, and Martin Weber, "The Curse of Knowledge in Economic Settings: An Experimental Analysis." PDF file. Journal of Political Economy 97, no. 5 (1989): 1232-1254. https://www.cmu.edu/dietrich/sds/docs/loewenstein/CurseknowledgeEconSet.pdf.

30 Jane Kennedy, "Debiasing the Curse of Knowledge in Audit Judgment," The Accounting Review 70, no. 2 (April 1995): 249-273.

31 Ellyn Shook and Julie Sweet, "Getting to Equal 2019: Creating a Culture That Drives Innovation," Accenture, accessed August 24, 2020, https://www.accenture.com/us-en/about/inclusion-diversity/gender-equality-innovation-research.

32 Shook and Sweet.

33 Rocío Lorenzo, et al., "The Mix That Matters: Innovation Through Diversity," Boston Consulting Group, April 26, 2017, https://www.bcg.com/publications/2017/people-organization-leadership-talent-innovation-through-diversity-mix-that-matters.

34 Lorenzo, et al., "The Mix that Matters."

35 Lorenzo, et al.

36 Lorenzo, et al.

37 Lorenzo, et al., "The Mix that Matters."

38 Lorenzo, et al.

39 Ben Schiller, "Want A More Innovative Company? Simple: Hire A More Diverse Workforce," Fast Company, January 12, 2018, https://www.fastcompany.com/40515712/want-a-more-innovative-company-simple-hire-a-more-diverse-workforce .

40 Schiller, "Want a More Innovative Company?"

41 Katharine Nester, "Diversity, Innovation and Opportunity: Why You Need A Diverse Product Engineering Team," Forbes, July 31, 2018, https://www.forbes.com/sites/forbestechcouncil/2018/07/31/diversity-innovation-and-opportunity-why-you-need-a-diverse-product-engineering-team/#5d63bd4f3e33.

42 Nester.

43 Shook and Sweet, "Getting to Equal 2019."

44 Shook and Sweet.

45 Shook and Sweet.

46 Shook and Sweet.

47 Rob Gonda, "Adaptability Is Key to Survival In the Age of Digital Darwinism," Forbes, May 24, 2018, https://www.forbes.com/sites/forbestechcouncil/2018/05/24/adaptability-is-key-to-survival-in-the-age-of-digital-darwinism/#5e094793408c.

48 Gonda.

49 Martin Reeves and Mike Deimler, "Adaptability: The New Competitive Advantage," Harvard Business Review, July 2011, https://hbr.org/2011/07/adaptability-the-new-competitive-advantage.

50 Bunkhuon Chhun, "Better Decisions Through Diversity," Kellogg Insights, October 1, 2010, https://insight.kellogg.northwestern.edu/article/better_decisions_through_diversity.

51 Chhun.

52 https://powerpastimpossible.org/stories/brainpower/

53 "About," Ruby, accessed August 23, 2020, https://www.ruby.com/about-ruby/.

54 Ruby.

55 "Race and Ethnic Standards for Federal Statistics and Administrative Reporting, " CDC, last modified November 19, 2019,

56 https://wonder.cdc.gov/wonder/help/populations/bridged-race/directive15.html.

57 Office of Management and Budget, "Revisions to the Standards for the Classification of Federal Data on Race and Ethnicity," Obama White House, accessed August 24, 2020, https://obamawhitehouse.archives.gov/omb/fedreg_1997standards

58 Office of Management and Budget.

59 Fan, "Proof that Diversity Drives Innovation."

60 Pamela Babcock, "5 Steps to Improve Diversity Recruiting," SHRM, February 24, 2017, https://www.shrm.org/resourcesandtools/hr-topics/talent-acquisition/pages/five-steps-improve-diversity-recruiting.aspx.

61 Billy Vaughn, "The Top Ten Culturally Competent Interviewing Strategies," Diversity Officer Magazine, accessed August 24, 2020, https://diversityofficermagazine.com/cultural-competence/the-top-ten-culturally-competent-interviewing-strategies/.

62 Livermore, Driven by Difference, 2.

63 Livermore, Driven by Difference, 239-244.

64 Livermore, 3.

65 P. Christopher Earley and Elaine Mosakowski, "Cultural Intelligence," Harvard Business Review, October 2004, https://hbr.org/2004/10/cultural-intelligence.

66 "About," Cultural Intelligence Center, accessed August 23, 2020, https://culturalq.com/about-cultural-intelligence/.

67 "Cultural Intelligence (CQ)," Business Dictionary, accessed August 23, 2020, http://www.businessdictionary.com/definition/cultural-intelligence-CQ.html.

68 Yasmine Yehia, "The Importance of Cultural Intelligence in International Business," Global Edge, February 16, 2018, https://globaledge.msu.edu/blog/post/55562/the-importance-of-cultural-intelligence.

69 Yehia, "The Importance of Cultural Intelligence."

70 Renee Navarro, "Unconscious Bias," University of California, San Francisco, accessed August 23, 2020, https://diversity.ucsf.edu/resources/unconscious-bias.

71 Christine Comaford, "How to Work with Unconscious Bias in your Organization," Forbes, June 25, 2016, https://www.forbes.com/sites/christinecomaford/2016/06/25/how-leaders-bust-unconscious-biases-in-business/#4e8e4d862c66.

72 Comaford.

73 Comaford, "How to Work with Unconscious Bias."

74 Tat Bellamy Walker and Richard Feloni, "Here's the presentation google gives employees on how to spot unconscious bias at work," Business Insider, June 8, 2020, https://www.businessinsider.com/google-unconscious-bias-training-presentation-2015-12.

75 Jon-Mark Sabel, "5 Steps to Reduce Bias in the Workplace." HireVue, April 23, 2018, https://www.hirevue.com/blog/5-steps-to-mitigating-bias-in-the-workplace.

76 Sabel, "5 Steps to Reduce Bias."

77 Harvard study.

78 "How to identify Hidden biases," CareerCast Diversity, accessed August 23, 2020, https://diversity.careercast.com/article/how-identify-hidden-biases.

79 Frank Dobbin, Alexandra Kalev, and Erin Kelly, "Diversity management in Corporate America," Contexts 6, no. 4 (Fall 2007): 21-27. https://scholar.harvard.edu/dobbin/files/2007_contexts_dobbin_kalev_kelly.pdf.

80 Dobbin, Kalev, and Kelly.

81 Charlotte Blank, "5 Ways to Tackle Bias in the Workplace," TLNT, July 20, 2018, https://www.tlnt.com/5-was-to-tackle-bias-in-the-workplace/.

82 Blank.

83 Blank, "5 Ways to Tackle Bias in the Workplace."

84 Alex Lindsay, et al., "The Impact of Method, Motivation, and Empathy on Diversity Training Effectiveness," Journal of Business Psychology 30 (2015): 605-617, https://doi.org/10.1007/s10869-014-9384-3.

85 Frans Johansson, The Medici Effect: Breakthroughs Insights at the Intersection of Ideas, Concepts, and Cultures (Cambridge: Harvard Business School Press, 2004).

86 Lloyd Mander, "Relational analytics: Ideation, innovation and diverse thinking," Diversity of thought blog, February 1, 2019, https://diversityofthought.co.nz/blog/f/relational-analytics-ideation-innovation-and-diverse-thinking.

87 Mander.

88 Mander.

89 Neal Ungerleider, "Startup Culture's Lack of Diversity Stifles Innovation," Fast Company, July 18, 2013, https://www.fastcompany.com/3014434/startup-cultures-lack-of-diversity-stifles-innovation.

90 "About the Diversity, Inc. top 50 Process," DiversityInc, accessed August 24, 2020, https://www.diversityinc.com/about-the-diversityinc-top-50-process/.

91 "Diversity and Inclusion," Mastercard, accessed August 24, 2020, https://www.mastercard.us/en-us/about-mastercard/who-we-are/diversity-inclusion.html.

92 Mastercard, "Diversity and Inclusion."

93 Mastercard.

94 Mastercard.

95 "Fortune 100 Best Companies to Work For® 2019," Great Place to Work, accessed August 24, 2020, https://www.greatplacetowork.com/best-workplaces/100-best/2019.

96 "Marriott International," DiversityInc, accessed August 24, 2020, https://www.diversityinc.com/marriott-international/.

97 Marriott.

98 "Accenture," DiversityInc, accessed August 24, 2020, https://www.diversityinc.com/accenture/.

99 DiversityInc, "Accenture."

100 DiversityInc, "Accenture."

101 "Home," Business for Trans Equality, accessed August 24, 2020, https://businessfortransequality.com/.

102 "Home," Employers for pay Equity, accessed August 24, 2020, http://www.employersforpayequity.com/.

103 "About," Paradigm for Parity, accessed August 24, 2020, https://www.paradigm4parity.com/about#who-we-are.

104 Johnson and Johnson, "Diversity & Inclusion."

105 "Hall of Fame | Johnson & Johnson," DiversityInc, accessed August 24, 2020, https://www.diversityinc.com/johnson-johnson-hall-of-fame/.

106 "Publix Makes Fortune's 100 Best Companies to Work For List for 23rd Straight Year," Publix, February 18, 2020, https://corporate.publix.com/about-publix/newsroom/news-releases/publix-makes-fortunes-100-best-companies-to-work-for-23-straight-years.

107 Hua Hsu, "The Year in 'Diversity Fatigue,'" The New Yorker, December 26, 2017, https://www.newyorker.com/culture/2017-in-review/the-year-in-diversity-fatigue.

108 "Diversity Fatigue in the Workplace: How to Get Unstuck," Catalyst, August 7, 2019, https://www.catalyst.org/2019/08/07/diversity-fatigue/.